The Writings of Frithjof Schuon

Series

World Wisdom
The Library of Perennial Philosophy

The Library of Perennial Philosophy is dedicated to the exposition of the timeless Truth underlying the diverse religions. This Truth, often referred to as the *Sophia Perennis*—or Perennial Wisdom—finds its expression in the revealed Scriptures as well as the writings of the great sages and the artistic creations of the traditional worlds.

The Perennial Philosophy provides the intellectual principles capable of explaining both the formal contradictions and the transcendent unity of the great religions.

Ranging from the writings of the great sages of the past, to the perennialist authors of our time, each series of our Library has a different focus. As a whole, they express the inner unanimity, transforming radiance, and irreplaceable values of the great spiritual traditions. *Adastra & Stella Maris* appears in our series entitled The Writings of Frithjof Schuon.

The Writings of Frithjof Schuon

The Writings of Frithjof Schuon series form the foundation of our library because he is the pre-eminent exponent of the Perennial Philosophy. His work illuminates this perspective in both an essential and comprehensive manner like none other.

Frithjof Schuon, 1907-1998, wrote more than twenty distinguished books on metaphysics and various world religions which have been translated into many languages. Concerning Schuon's writings, Huston Smith has written: "The man is a living wonder; intellectually apropos religion,equally in breadth and depth, the paragon of our time."

Adastra
& Stella Maris

Poems by
Frithjof Schuon

German-English Edition

Foreword by
Annemarie Schimmel

World Wisdom

Adastra and Stella Maris
Poems by Frithjof Schuon
©2003 World Wisdom, Inc.

Library of Congress Cataloging-in-Publication Data

Schuon, Frithjof, 1907-1998
  Adastra ; Stella Maris : poems / by Frithjof Schuon ; foreword by Annemarie
  Schimmel.-- German-English ed.
    p. cm. -- (Library of perennial philosophy) (The writings of Frithjof Schuon)

ISBN 0-941532-56-9 (pbk. : alk. paper)
  I. Title: Adastra ; Stella Maris. II. Schuon, Frithjof, 1907-1998 Stella Maris. III.
  Schimmel, Annemarie. IV. Title: Stella Maris. V. Title. VI.

Series.
  PT2680.U474A2 2003
  831'.92--dc22

                                                            2003018957

Cover art: Detail from a painting by Frithjof Schuon

Printed on acid-free paper in Canada

For information address World Wisdom, Inc.
P.O. Box 2682, Bloomington, Indiana 47402-2682

www.worldwisdom.com

Contents

Frithjof Schuon

Foreword

It seems that mystical experience almost inevitably leads to poetry. The great mystics all over the world used the language of poetry when trying to beckon to a mystery that lies beyond normal human experience, and the most glorious works in Eastern and Western religions are the hymns of the mystics, be they Sufis or Christians, Hindus or Zen monks. Different as their expressions are, one feels that the poetical word can more easily lead to the mystery that is hidden behind the veils of intellectual knowledge and which cannot be fettered in logical speech.

In the world of Islam, the love-intoxicated poems of Maulana Jalaladdin Rumi are considered by many to be "the Koran in the Persian tongue," and Rumi is only one of many intoxicated souls who expressed their love and longing, and their experience of the Divine Unity, in verse. And even those mystics who preferred a more "intellectual" approach to the Absolute couched their experiences in verse. The prime example is, of course, Ibn Arabi whose *Tarjuman al-ashwaq* translated his experience of the One, Unattainable Deity into the language of traditional Arabic poetry.

Taking this fact into consideration we are not surprised that Frithjof Schuon too felt compelled to write poetry—and, it is important to note, poetry in his German mother tongue. His verse sometimes reflects ideas and images of R. M. Rilke's *Stundenbuch*, in which the expert on mysticism can find some strange echoes of Ibn Arabi's ideas. This may be an accident, for mystical ideas are similar all over the world; but the German reader of Schuon's verses enjoys the familiar sound. This sound could not be maintained in the English translations of his poetry. Yet, as he himself explains, what really matters is the content, and here we listen to the thinker who, far from the intricate and complex scholarly sentences of his learned prose works, sings the simple prayers of the longing soul: God is the center, the primordial ground which comprehends everything, manifesting Himself through the colorful play of His creations. And it is the human heart which alone can reflect the incomprehensible Being, for humanity's central quality is divinely inspired love, which is the axis of our life.

I hope that Schuon's mystical verse will be read not only by English speaking readers but even more by those who understand German. They will enjoy many of these tender lyrics which show the famous thinker in a very different light and from an unexpected side.

—Annemarie Schimmel, Professor Emeritus, Harvard University

Introduction

Frithjof Schuon (1907-1998) was a sage, an artist, and a poet. During the last three years of his life, he wrote in German—his mother tongue—approximately 3,500 short poems, in 23 separate collections. A start has now been made to publish these poems, along with their translation into English. The present book contains the first two collections, *Adastra* and *Stella Maris*.

The words *ad astra* ("to the stars") first appear in the Sixth Book of Virgil's *Aeneid*: *Macte novā virtute, puer, sic itur ad astra* ("Good speed to thy youthful valor, child, thus wilt thou journey to the stars!"). The words also appear in Seneca's phrase: *Per aspera ad astra* ("Through difficulties to the stars"). Frithjof Schuon uses the form *Adastra* to signify spiritual striving. The term *Stella Maris* ("Star of the Sea") is a title accorded by the Christian tradition to the Holy Virgin.

In content, Schuon's German poems are similar to those in his English collection *Road to the Heart*, but they are much more numerous, and the imagery is even more rich and powerful. The poems cover every possible aspect of metaphysical doctrine, spiritual method, spiritual virtue, and the role and function of beauty. They express every conceivable subtlety of spiritual and moral counsel—and this not merely in general terms, but with uncanny intimacy, detail and precision. They exhibit incredible sharpness, profundity, comprehensiveness, and compassion.

Some of the poems are autobiographical, with reminiscences of places experienced: Basle and Paris, the fairy-tale streets of old German towns, Morocco and Andalusia, Turkey and Greece, the American West. Others evoke the genius of certain peoples, such as the Hindus, the Japanese, the Arabs, the American Indians, and also the Cossacks and the Gypsies. Yet other poems elucidate the rôle of music, dance, and poetry itself. In one or two poems, the godless modern world comes in for biting, and sometimes fiercely humorous, comment:

A worldly banquet: chandeliers glitter
    In the large hall —
And brilliant society, ladies and gentlemen
    Sit down for the meal.
They talk of everything and they talk of nothing —
    The wine is red,
And so are the flowers.
        But no one, no one
    Thinks of death.

The poems embody both severity and compassion. They are powerfully interiorizing. The author repeatedly demonstrates the link between truth, prayer, virtue and beauty. For him these are the four things needful; they are the very purpose of life, the only source of happiness, and the essential means of salvation. They are the panacea (*panakeia*), the remedy for all ills:

Why has God given us the gift of speech?
    For prayer.
Because God's blessing enters the heart of him
    Who trusts in God.

The very first cry in this life
    Is a prayer.
And the last breath is a word of hope —
    Given by God.

What is the substance of which man is made,
    His deepest I?
It is the Word that grants us salvation:
    Lord, hear me!

Many of the poems express the purpose of life with unmistakable clarity, for example:

All creatures exist in order to say "God";
So must thou too accept the world's vocation,
O man, who art king of the earth —

Woe unto him who forgets the kernel of his existence;
No animal, no plant nor stone does this;
But only man, with his free will,
In his madness.
　　　　　Say "God" throughout thy life;
It will be a grace for others too.

For an aura radiates from the Supreme Name —
Prayer is blessing; it is the seed of the Divine.

No translation can possibly do full justice to the "poetry"—the meter, rhyme, verbal appositeness, allusions, music, inspiration—of the original German. Each German poem is a diamond—sparkling and clear, an architectural masterpiece full of light.

In his rich profusion of references to the many and varied cultural forms of Europe and beyond—the streets of the Latin Quarter, Andalusian nights, la Virgen del Pilar, la Macarena, sages such as Dante, Shankara, Pythagoras and Plato, the Psalms of David, Arab wisdom, the graces of the Bodhisattvas, Tibetan prayer-wheels, Samurai and Shinto, the songs of love and longing of many peoples—in all of these diverse cultures, Schuon captures the timeless message of truth and beauty which each contains, and renders it present in a most joyful way. When these cultural forms happen to be ones that the reader himself has known and loved, the joy that emanates from the poems is great indeed.

Schuon's long cycle of poems has already been compared to Rumi's *Mathnawī*. I think that many of his poems can also be compared to the Psalms of David: they are an expression of nostalgia, of mankind's longing for, and ultimate satisfaction in, the Lord. Their main theme is trustful prayer to an ever-merciful God, and benevolence towards men of goodwill. First and foremost, the poems are instruments of instruction. As such, they are a powerful propulsion towards the inward.

A blessing lies not only in the quality of the poems, but also in the quantity—they constitute an all-inclusive totality. On the one hand, Schuon's German poems recapitulate the teachings contained in his philosophical works in French; on the other, they are an inexhaustible, and ever new, purifying fountain—a crystalline and living expression of the *Religio perennis*. They epitomize truth, beauty, and salvation.

—William Stoddart

Adastra

Ein Liederkranz

A Garland of Songs

Zum Eingang

Es floss aus meinem Herzen mancher Sang;
Ich sucht ihn nicht, er ward mir eingegeben.
O mög der gottgeschenkten Harfe Klang
Die Seele läutern, uns zum Himmel heben —

Möge das Licht der Wahrheit sich verbinden
Mit Liebe, unsrem Streben zum Geleit;
Und mögen unsre Seelen Gnade finden —

Den Weg von Gott zu Gott — in Ewigkeit.

Adastra

Ad astra — zu den Sternen — strebt die Seele,
Die eine ungestillte Sehnsucht drängt.
O Weg der Wahrheit, Schönheit, den ich wähle —
Des Gottgedenkens, das die Seele tränkt.

Du bist das Lied, das alles Sehnen stillt —
Das Gnadenlicht; schein in das Herz hinein!
Der Herr ist unsre Zuflucht, unser Schild —

Sei du mit Ihm, und Er wird mit dir sein.

As an Entry

Out of my heart flowed many songs;
I sought them not, they were inspired in me.
O may the sound of the God-given harp
Purify the soul and raise us to Heaven —

May the light of Truth unite
With love to accompany our striving,
And may our souls find grace —

The path from God to God — in eternity.

Adastra

Ad astra — to the stars — the soul is striving,
Called by an unstilled longing.
O path of Truth and Beauty that I choose —
Of God-remembrance that pervades the soul!

Thou art the song that stills all longing —
The Light of Grace; shine into my heart!
The Lord is our Refuge, our Shield —

Be thou with Him, and He will be with thee.

Memento

Wenn du auf Gottes Boden stehst,
Wenn du auf Gottes Wege gehst,
Bedaure niemals, was vergeht —
Die Träume, die der Wind verweht.

Der Wahrheit Boden schwanket nicht;
Der Weg des Heils ist Trost und Licht.
Vor Falschem mach die Augen zu;
Im Wahren ist der Seele Ruh.

Wohl dem, der sich nicht täuschen lässt;
Auf einem Felsen steht er fest.
Auf deinem Weg schau nicht zurück;
Denn zeitlos ist des Herzens Glück.

Es kann nicht anders sein: es muss
Auch Arges geben und Verdruss.
Der Allerhöchste sei dein Hort;
Der Liebe ist das letzte Wort.

Wahrheit und Treue sind die Kraft
Die alles Gute wirkt und schafft.
Kampf ist wohl das Gesetz der Zeit;
Von Frieden singt die Ewigkeit.

Wahrheit und Treu sind eine Macht,
Daraus ist unser Herz gemacht.
Und Licht und Liebe sind ein Sang
Der vor der Zeit in Gott erklang.

Memento

When thou art standing on God's ground,
When thou art walking on God's path,
Never regret what is fleeting —
Dreams the wind sweeps away.

The ground of Truth can never falter,
The path of salvation is solace and light.
Before falsehood close thine eyes;
The soul's repose lies in the True.

Blest is he who is not deceived;
He stands fast upon a rock.
On thy way do not look back;
For timeless is the heart's happiness.

It cannot be otherwise:
Wrongs and vexations must exist.
Let the Most High be thy Refuge;
The final word belongs to Love.

Truth and faithfulness are the force
That begets all good and makes it prosper.
Struggle is indeed the law of time;
Eternity sings of Peace.

Truth and faithfulness are a power
Of which our heart is made.
And Light and Love are a song
That resounded in God, before time began.

Serenitas

Bei Gott, dem Höchsten Gut, bist du geborgen.
Des Bösen Werk ist eitel Trug und Schein.
So lass den Kummer, mach dir keine Sorgen.
Sei du bei Gott, und Er wird bei dir sein.

Nie sollst du deinen Blick vom Einen wenden;
Es ist des Lebens Zweck und Sinn.
Das Weltgetriebe ist in Gottes Händen
Und nicht in deiner Macht; schau du nicht hin.

Zuerst Ergebenheit, dann Gottvertrauen;
Der Weg zu Gott ist nicht so weit.
So magst du, Seele, in die Zukunft schauen —
Und in das Licht der Ewigkeit.

Veritas

Zuerst die Wahrheit, die uns alles klärt;
Dann unser Werden, was die Wahrheit kündet.
Und dann der Name, der mit Licht uns nährt —
Dann auch die Schönheit, die ins Eine mündet.

Sei du bei Gott, und Gott wird bei dir sein;
Nie sollst du deinen Blick vom Einen wenden.
Die Wahrheit wirkt in deines Herzens Schrein —

Und alles andre ist in Gottes Händen.

Serenitas

In God, the Sovereign Good, thou art secure;
The Enemy's work is but a vain delusion.
So leave aside thy care, be not distressed;
Be thou with God, and He will be with thee.

Turn not thy gaze from Him who is the One;
He is the aim and meaning of thy life.
The turmoil of the world is in God's Hands,
Not in thy power; pay no heed to it.

First resignation, and then trust in God;
The way to God is not so far.
May thou, O soul, look toward the future —
And toward the radiance of Eternity.

Veritas

First the Truth, that clarifies all things;
Then our becoming what the Truth proclaims.
And then the Name that nourishes with Light —
Then Beauty, flowing back into the One.

Be thou with God, and God will be with thee;
Turn not thy gaze from Him who is the One.
The living Truth will act in thy heart's shrine —

All else lies in the Hands of God.

Die Burg

Die Wahrheit ist die feste Burg;
Im Wahren sollst du wohnen.
Beim Morgengrauen denke dran;
Der Abend wird dir's lohnen.

Der Erdenkram, der macht dich schwer
Mit eitlem Traumgewebe.
Die Seel ist müd; der Geist ist wach,
Dass er nach Oben schwebe.

Das Rätsel

Das Weltmeer, mit dem Guten und dem Bösen,
Der Erdenkram mit seiner falschen Fülle
Und seinem Lärm; wer kann das Rätsel lösen?
Sei ruhig, Herz; steh du in Gottes Stille.

Nicht weltlich ist, was unterm Himmelszelt
Von Eden zeugt; dass sich dein Geist nicht quäle:
Das Schöne ist nicht ganz von dieser Welt.

Es ist von Gott zu Gott — wie deine Seele.

The Fortress

Truth is the mighty fortress;
In the True thou shouldst abide.
At early dawn recall it,
And evening will reward thee.

Earthly trifles weigh thee down
In an idle web of dreams.
The soul is weary; the spirit wakes,
That it may soar aloft.

The Enigma

The world-sea, with its good and bad,
Earthly vanity with its false plenitude
And din; who can resolve the enigma?
Be still, my heart; abide in the Silence of God.

Under heaven's vault, what bears witness to Eden
Is not worldly; let not thy mind torment thee:
Beauty is not wholly of this world.

It is from God to God — like thine own soul.

Kosmos

Da wo das Lichte erscheinet,
    Da muss auch das Finstere drohen;
Wundre und gräme dich nicht;
    So will es das wirkende Sein.
Siehe, die niederen Mächte
    Bekämpfen heimtückisch die hohen;
Da wo ein Abel erstrahlet,
    Da ist auch ein finsterer Kain.

Denn die Allmöglichkeit Gottes
    Erfordert ja auch die Verneinung:
Wahrheit und Friede sind himmlisch,
    Irdisch sind Falschheit und Krieg.
Ohne das Übel der Trennung,
    Wo wäre das Gut der Vereinung?
Ohne der Finsternis Treiben,
    Wo wäre der Trost und der Sieg?

Geheimnis

Ich muss wohl der sein, der ich bin, mein Gott —
    Wär ich ein andrer,
Ich wäre doch in dieser weiten Welt
    Derselbe Wandrer.

Gar selten ist das Menschenkind, das Dem
    Was sein muss, glich —
Du, Herr, schaust auf der Seelen wechselnd Spiel —
    Nur Du bist Ich.

Geschrieben steht: Der Herr ist unser Hirt —
Du weißt, o Herz, dass dir nichts mangeln wird.

Cosmos

Wherever light appears
    Darkness must also threaten;
Do not wonder and grieve,
    Existence will have it thus.
See how the lower powers
    Maliciously battle the higher;
Wherever Abel shines,
    There also is dark Cain.

For God's All-Possibility
    Also demands negation:
Truth and Peace are of Heaven,
    Earthly are falsehood and war.
Without the evil of separation,
    Where would be the good of reunion?
Without the work of darkness,
    Where would be solace and victory?

Mystery

My God, I must indeed be who I am —
    If I were someone else
I still would be, in this vast world,
    The self-same wanderer.

Rare is the human being who resembles That
    Which must be —
Thou, O Lord, lookest on the changing play of souls —
    Thou alone art "I."

It is written: the Lord is our Shepherd —
Thou knowest, O heart, that thou shalt not want.

Zeitlied

Du drehst dich, Weltrad, tiefer Urgesang
Des Kommens, Gehens, manch Jahrtausend lang.
Gar manches Dasein blühte über Nacht,
Das du ins kalte Nichts zurückgebracht.

So drehst dich, Weltrad, bis des Höchsten Hand
Dich an des Zyklus Ende festgebannt;
Dein Sang verrauscht, verstummt in letzter Stille —
Nur eins verharrt:
Des Wandellosen Wille.

Weltrad

Auch wenn es sich in tiefsten Schlaf verlor —
Das Weltrad steigt aufs Neu zum Sein empor,
Es schöpft, vernichtet, steht nicht ewig still;
Es muss sein, was es ist —
Wie Gott es will.

Möglichkeit

Nur Möglichkeit sind wir, und nicht wie Gott
Notwendigkeit; sie kann uns nicht gehören.
Wir können ihr gehören, so sie will;
Dann kann uns nimmer das Vielleicht betören.

Dann ist es Gottes Sein, das in uns wirkt,
Und unsre Ichheit ist bloß Daseinshülle
Im Reich der Zeit. Wolle die Vorsehung
Dass, was wir sind, des Daseins Sinn erfülle.

Song of Time

World-wheel, deep primordial song of coming and going,
Thou turnest for eons, on and on.
Countless existences that blossomed overnight,
Hast thou brought back to coldest naught.

So thou turnest, world-wheel, till the Hand of the Most High
Brings thee to a halt at cycle's end.
Thy song now hushed, fading in ultimate silence,
One thing alone remains:
                    the Will of Him who does not change.

World Wheel

Even when lost in deepest sleep —
The world-wheel rises again to being,
Creating, destroying, never standing still;
It must be what it is —
                    According to God's Will.

Possibility

We are but possibility, and not, like God,
Necessity, which cannot belong to us.
We can belong to it, if it so wills,
Then we are no longer deluded by "perhaps."

It is then God's Being that works through us,
And our ego is a mere husk of existence
In the realm of time. May Providence ordain
That what we are fulfill the meaning of our existence.

Verbindung

Der weise Mensch, der edle Mensch: sie beide
Sollten in jeder Seele sich befinden.
Der Weise schaut nach Innen, nach dem Sein;
Der Edle muss sich mit der Welt verbinden.

Denn ob wir wollen oder nicht, wir leben
In dieser Welt und unter andern Wesen —
Wir sind Verwandte, müssen unser Ich
Auch in der Selbstheit andrer Menschen lesen.

Weisheit wohnt auch in Māyā — im Gemüt;
Und Adel ist im Geist, der Ātmā sieht.

Gnade

Was heißt es denn: du bist in Gottes Händen?
Heißt es, dass Gott dein Schicksal hat bestimmt?
Gott wollte, dass du frei entscheiden mögest,
Was von der Seel die Last der Torheit nimmt.

In der Allmöglichkeit erschuf der Mensch
Sich selbst: er ist das, was er wollte sein.
Er wollte sich mit allen Folgerungen —
Jedoch: die Gnade kommt von Gott allein.

Barmherzigkeit, die Dasein's Rätsel rundet:
Einmal Gesetz, dann wieder freie Güte,
Die nichts berechnet — wie ein Regenschauer,
Der Leben bringt und Höchstes Gut bekundet —

So wollte Gott, dass Liebe uns behüte.

Association

The wise man and the noble man,
Both should be present in each soul.
The wise man looks inward, toward Being,
The noble man must be in contact with the world.

Whether we like it or not, we live
In this world and among other beings —
We are brethren, and we must see
Our own "I" in the self of other men.

Also in *Māyā* Wisdom dwells — in our soul;
The noble mind sees *Ātmā* in all things.

Grace

What does it mean that thou art in God's Hands?
Does it mean that God has ordained thy fate?
God's will is that thou shouldst freely decide
What liberates thy soul from folly's weight.

Within All-Possibility, man created himself:
He is what he wished to be.
He wished his self with all the consequences —
But grace comes from the Lord alone.

O mercy, resolving the riddle of existence,
Now law, now free compassion
Unaccounted for — like a rainshower
That bringing life proclaims the Highest Good.

For God so willed that Love protect us.

Gerechtigkeit

Wie schaut die Gottheit auf des Menschen Sünde?
Die Wahrheit richtet; Schönheit will vergeben.
Gewiss, die Missetat ist, was sie ist;
Doch gibt es in der Seel ein tiefres Leben.

Wenn unsre Sünden Gottes Zorn entzünden,
Kann trotzdem Gott sein Recht mit Lieb verbinden.
Wähnt nicht, des Seins Gerechtigkeit sei blind —
Sie schaut auf das, was wir im Grunde sind.

Gebe der Herr, dass kalter Rechnung Strenge
Durchkreuzt sei durch erlösende Gesänge
Der Liebe, die vor seinem Zorne tief
Sein Wesen war, und ist, und die uns rief.

Mag sein, dass Allbekanntes ich verkünde:
Den Seelengrund berührt nicht jede Sünde.

Kundgebung

Gott hat sich kundgegeben;
       Dies ist der Schöpfung Wert.
Kundgebung ist Entfernung;
       Der Strahl bleibt unversehrt.

Gott hat das Sein getrieben
       Tief in das Nichts hinein.
Und dennoch steht geschrieben:
       Welt kann nicht göttlich sein.

Das Herz will heilig werden
       Und steht vor Gottes Tür.
Ist Paradies auf Erden,
       Dann ist es hier, ja hier.

Justice

How does God look upon man's sin?
Truth judges; beauty wishes to forgive.
Misdeeds are clearly what they are,
But in the soul there is a deeper life.

When our sins inflame God's Wrath,
God still combines His Justice with His Love.
Deem not His Justice to be blind —
It looks at what we are in depth.

God grant that the cold severity of reckoning
Be countered by redeeming songs of Love;
The Love that was and is, before His Wrath,
Deep within His Being, and by it we are called to Him.

It may be I proclaim things widely known:
Not every sin touches the bottom of the soul.

Manifestation

God has manifested Himself;
        This is the value of Creation.
Manifestation means separation;
        The Divine Ray remains untouched.

God has driven Being
        Deeply into nothingness.
And yet it is written:
        World cannot be divine.

The heart wants to be holy
        And stands before God's gate.
If there is a Paradise on earth,
        It is here, yea, here.

Die Frage

Was kann den Menschen von der Welt befreien?
Es heißt, es sei die Frage, wer wir sind.
Sie mag wohl Wissen in die Seele streuen;
Doch ohne Gottheit geht sie in den Wind.

Denn ohne Gott, was kann das Denken tun?
Was wäre Weisheit, wenn ich Ihn nicht riefe?
In Seiner Gnade muss die Seele ruhn.

Was uns befreit, ist Gott in unsrer Tiefe.

Der Schleier

Traumschleier Welt: wer kann dein Spiel verstehen?
Ein Wunderwerk aus tausend Traumgeweben,
Oft wild bewegt wenn Schicksals Winde wehen;
Wer kann der dunklen Isis Schleier heben?

Denn dies Gewand verbirgt und offenbart;
Du siehst nicht das Geheimnis, doch der Wille
Des Schöpfers zeigt sich in der bunten Fülle,
Die sich um unsichtbare Mitte schart.

Was ist in alledem der letzte Sinn?
Die Äußerung zur Innerung: wir sollen
Bewirken, wenn des Daseins Bilder rollen,
Dass sie uns — gebe Gott — nach Innen ziehn.

Woher wir kommen und wohin wir gehen
In dieser Träumerei? Du sollst nicht fragen.
Das Weltrad mag sich um das Eine drehen —
Dieweil wir letztes Sein im Herzen tragen.

The Question

What liberates man from the world?
It is the question, it is said, of who we are.
This may well sow some wisdom in the soul,
But without God it is as fleeting as the wind.

For without God, what can thinking achieve?
What would wisdom be, if I did not call Him?
In His grace the soul should repose.

What liberates us, is God in our very depths.

The Veil

Dream-veil world: who can understand thy play?
A wonder-work woven of a thousand dreams,
So often wildly stirred when the winds of destiny blow;
Who can lift the veil of the dark Isis?

For this garment at once covers and reveals;
Thou canst not see the secret; but the Creator's
Will shows Itself in the colorful fullness
That gathers round the unseen Center.

What is the ultimate meaning in this?
Outwardness in view of inwardness;
As the images of existense roll past,
We must cause them — God willing — to draw us inward.

Whence do we come, and whither do we go
In all this dreaming? Thou shouldst not ask.
The world-wheel may circle round the One —
While we carry ultimate Being in our heart.

Wiederkehr

Dasein, dann nicht mehr dasein; Wirklichkeit,
Und nachher nichts; ein Trost, der von uns schied,
So wie ein ungehörtes Liebeslied
Im Zeichen eilender Vergänglichkeit
Bei Nacht verklingt.

            Jedoch ein Weiser sprach:
Du trauerst, weil die Welt verwelkt; sei wach
Und klage nicht; denn Gott enttäuscht uns nie.
Bei Ihm ist alles, was der Liebe wert,
Und was in neuer Strahlung wiederkehrt —
Ja aller Schönheit tiefste Melodie.

Und wisse: alles Gute, das vergeht,
Ist so beschaffen, dass es aufersteht.

Ātmā

Was du auch lieben magst, du liebst das Selbst
           Das in dir wohnt;
In jeder Liebe liebest du das Gut
           Das Oben thront;
Und es gehört zu deinem Seelenheil
           Dass du es weißt;
Und dass in jeder Lieb dein tiefstes Herz
           Den Höchsten preist.

Return

To exist, then to exist no more; reality,
Then nothing; a solace that has left us,
Just as a love song never heard
Marked by the sign of fleeting transcience
Dies away in the night.

                    And yet a wise man said:
You mourn because the world is fading; be wakeful
And lament not, for God never fails.
With Him is all that is worthy of love,
And that returns in new radiance —
Yea, all beauty's deepest melody.

And know: all good that passes away
Is so made that it rises again.

Ātmā

Whatever thou mayest love, thou lovest the Self
                    That dwells in thee;
In every love, thou lovest the Good
                    That is enthroned Above.
Part of thy soul's salvation is
                    That thou know this,
And that in every love thy deepest heart
                    Praise the Most High.

Mahnung

Du Erdenmensch, sei weise; warte nicht
Bis dir ein Gram der Welt das Herz zerbricht;
Gib es dem Allerhöchsten; es wird leben —
Er wird dein Herz in goldne Höhe heben.

Du Erdenmensch, sei weise; denn es hieß:
Hienieden ist für dich ein Paradies.
So bete: ich bin klein, mein Herz ist rein;
Du wirst mit einem Fuß im Himmel sein.

Die Laute

Da wo die Weisheit ist von Gott und Welt,
Da wo das Wort ist, Wissensdrang zu stillen:
Da muss die Laute sein mit ihrem Sang,
Die Seele mit der Schönheit Trost zu füllen —

Doch ohne Torheit; mit dem Widerschein
Von Engeln, tanzend auf der Himmelswiese.
Die Weisheit, rein und klar wie Bergkristall —
Mit ihr der Liebesklang vom Paradiese.

Ein Tanz, begleitet von der Laute Spiel,
Und Sehnsuchtslieder, die das Herz bewegen —
Wohl Weltlichkeit, wer weiß? Es könnte sein —
Oder auch Tiefenschau mit Gottes Segen.

Denn in der Schönheit wundersamen Raum,
Da findest du, was Menschenkinder wählen:
Für Toren Zeitvertreib und eitle Lust —

Der Andacht Licht erblüht in reinen Seelen.

Warning

Thou, earthly man, be wise; and do not wait
Until thy heart be broken by some sorrow deep;
Give it to the Most High and it will live —
He will lift up thy heart to golden heights.

Thou, earthly man, be wise; for it is said:
Here-below is a Paradise for thee.
So pray: "I am small, my heart is pure";
And with one foot in Heaven thou shalt be.

The Lute

Where there is wisdom of God and the world,
And the Word that stills the thirst for knowledge:
There must the lute be with its song,
To fill the soul with beauty's solace —

But without foolishness; with the reflection
Of angels dancing on the meadows of Heaven.
Wisdom, pure and clear like mountain crystal —
And with it the music of love from Paradise.

A dance accompanied by the lute,
And nostalgic songs that stir the heart —
It could be worldliness, who knows? Perhaps —
Or else deep vision, with God's blessing.

For within beauty's wondrous framework,
Thou wilt find what human beings choose:
For fools, mere pastime and pleasure-seeking —

In pure souls the light of devotion blooms.

Blumen

Was ist wohl eure Sprache, stumme Blumen,
Die ihr so freudig meine Wiese schmückt?
Wer hat euch aus dem grünen Gras gehoben,
Dass ihr mein Auge und mein Herz beglückt?

Da sind die roten und die blauen Sterne,
Der Wiese Frühlings- oder Sommerkleid;
Da sind die vielen weißen Perlen, schimmernd
Wie Schnee, über die Gräser hingestreut.

Wohlan, es wollte auch die Erde singen:
Sie wollte Liebeslied und Laute sein,
So wie die Vögel, hoch mit ihren Schwingen —
So wie zuhöchst des Himmels Engelein.

Seligkeit

Der Ort der Seligkeit ist eine Stadt —
So ward gelehrt — gemacht aus Edelsteinen,
Mit Märchenbauten, schimmernden Palästen
Und Tempeln, die im reinsten Golde scheinen;

Für andre ist der Ort ein Paradies:
Die Selgen hören Harfenspiel und schauen
Auf Blütenbäume, darin Vöglein singen,
Auf Lotosteiche und auf nackte Frauen.

Es kann nichts besseres beschrieben werden
In Menschenworten; denn unendlich mehr
Ist Seligkeit, als was erscheint auf Erden.

Flowers

What are you saying, silent flowers,
Joyfully adorning my meadow?
Who raised you out of the green grass,
To give my eyes and heart delight?

Here are red stars, and there are blue,
The meadow's spring or summer dress;
And here are numberless white pearls,
Gleaming like snow, and strewn across the grass.

It seems the earth too wished to sing,
She wished to be a lovesong and a lute,
Like birds, high-soaring on their wings —
And, highest of all, like little angels from Heaven.

Beatitude

The place of felicity — we are told —
Is like a city made of precious stones,
With fairy-tale buildings, glittering palaces
And temples that shine in purest gold.

For others, paradise is a place where
Blessèd souls listen to the sound of harps,
And gaze on trees in flower where birds sing,
On lotus ponds and on naked women.

This cannot better be described
By words, for bliss is infinitely more
Than what appears on earth.

Vom Lieben

Tatsächlich liebt der eine Mensch den andern;
Grundsätzlich liebt er Gott, und weiß es nicht;
Oder er weiß es. Heilig ist die Lieb,
Weil in ihr schläft der Gottesminne Licht.

Besinnung

Gespräch mit Gott. Er wird dir Antwort geben,
Oder sein Schweigen wird dir Antwort sein;
Denn Er ist bei dir; du bist nie allein.
In seiner Stille mag dein Herz erbeben —

Und lauschen, was der Name Gottes spricht.
Du ahnest, wie des Himmels Gärten blühen;
Du hörst des Urseins tiefe Melodien —

Den Urgesang von Liebe und von Licht.

Loving

When one human being loves another,
In reality he loves God and does not know it;
Or he does know. Holy is love,
For in it sleeps the light of Divine Love.

Meditation

Talk to God. He will answer thee,
Or else His Silence will be an answer;
For He is with thee; thou art never alone.
In His Stillness may thy heart be stirred —

And listen to what the Name of God is saying:
Thou canst divine how Heaven's gardens bloom;
Thou hearest the deep melodies of primordial Being —

The primal song of Love and Light.

Der Tanz

Traumschleier Welt: wer hat dich so gewoben
Wie du, in deiner zauberhaften Pracht
Das Nichts durchbrichst? Wer hat den Traum erdacht —
Bald siegreich, bald gebrochen und zerstoben?

Traumschleier Raum und Zeit: bald Lust, bald Leid;
Der Schleier tanzt, bewegt und wendet sich,
Deckt und enthüllt der Māyā nacktes Ich —

O goldne Strahlung der Unendlichkeit!

Der Tod

Ihr denkt mit falschem Sinnen an den Tod.
Ihr wähnt, der Tod sei nur das dunkle Ende,
Das alles auslöscht; Lebens letzte Not.

Bedenkt: das Sterben ist die große Wende;
Es ist die Türe zur Unsterblichkeit.
Es muss so sein, das zeiget unser Streben
Zum Ewigen; das zeiget unser Geist,
Des Wesen uns beweist: der Tod bringt Leben.

Der Mensch kann es im Herzen fühlen, wenn
Die Stunde schlägt. Wer um das Höchste wirbt,
Der weiß: der Weise stirbt bevor er stirbt.

„Die Saat bringt keine Frucht, sie sterbe denn."

Dance

Dream-veil world: who wove thee thus,
As thou, in thine enthralling splendor,
Piercest the naught? Who conceived this dream —
Now victorious, now shattered and dispelled?

Dream-veil space and time: now joy, now grief;
The veil dances, moves and whirls,
Covers and uncovers *Māyā*'s naked self —

O golden radiance of Infinity!

Death

You think of death with false conception.
You deem it to be merely the dark end
Erasing everything; this life's last misery.

But rather think: death is the great change;
It is the door to immortality.
It must be so; it is shown by our striving
Toward Eternity, and by our spirit,
Whose nature is the proof that death brings life.

Man feels it in his heart when his last hour
Tolls. The one who seeks the Most High knows:
The wise man dies before he dies.

"Except it die, the seed will bear no fruit."

Ichheit

Beim Rätsel „ich" hat oft mein Sinn geweilt.
Warum bin ich es, der für „ich" sich hält,
Und nicht ein andrer? Warum ist die Welt
In viele tausend Spiegel aufgeteilt?

Doch siehe: niemand ist erstaunt darüber.
Man lebt blindlings in den Tag hinein
Und denkt an manches, nur an dieses nicht;
Man meint getrost: es kann nicht anders sein.

Und dies ist seltsam: dass das Ich sich färbt
Je nach dem Alter, je nach dem Erleben;
Wer bin ich denn? Wer hat mein Herz geerbt,
Wer kann mein Ich aus seinem Kreislauf heben?

Und hinter allem thront das Eine Selbst,
Zutiefst verborgne Sonne unter Schalen
Des Erdenseins.
                    Sonne, mögest Du
In unsrer Ichheit dunkle Kammer strahlen!

"I-ness"

My mind has often dwelt on the enigma "I."
Why is it I who thinks himself "I,"
And not another? Why is the world
Divided into many thousand mirrors?

Yet see: no one wonders at it.
One blindly lives throughout the day
And thinks on many things, but not on this;
One readily believes it cannot be otherwise.

And this is strange: the I is colored
According to age, according to experience;
Who am I then? Who has inherited my heart,
Who can lift my I out of its orbit?

And behind all is enthroned the Unique Self,
Deep-hidden Sun beneath the shell
Of earthly existence.
           O Sun, mayest Thou shine
Into the somber cell of our "I-ness"!

Der Zorn

Drei Triebe hegt das weite Weltgewebe:
Lichtstrahlend, lebensglühend, schwer und dunkel;
Dann auch gemischt, ein trügendes Gefunkel;
Bedenke, Mensch, wohin die Seele strebe.

Und siehe, wie der Herr die Herzen wägt
Und wie sein Licht die Finsternis besiegt;
Und wisse, dass sein Zorn das Böse schlägt,
Weil dies in dessen eignem Wesen liegt.

Gewiss: das Aufwärts hat das letzte Wort,
Das Abwärts kann nicht dauernd überwiegen.
O Menschen, lasst die Torheit, strebet fort —
So wie der Sonne zu die Adler fliegen.

Unsterblichkeit

Wie kannst du wirklich nennen, was einst war
Und nicht mehr ist; des Schicksals Zauberei,
Die wie ein Lied über die Leyer ging —
Ein Saitenspiel der Zeit; vorbei, vorbei.

Vergänglich nennst du, was im Lebenstraum
Einst sterblich war, doch dann zum Sein erwachte:
Die Seele, die der Schöpfer ewig machte,
Bevor sie wanderte durch Zeit und Raum.

Glückselig jener, den die Wahrheit küsst,
Der Gottes Absicht in den Dingen findet.
Man liebt das Schöne, weil es Gott verkündet;
Man liebt es, weil es tief und ewig ist.

Wrath

Three forces move the vast fabric of the world:
Radiating light, glowing life, and heavy darkness;
Then also mingled, a deceptive glitter;
Consider, man, whither thy soul is going.

Behold the way the Lord weighs hearts,
How His Light overcomes the dark.
And know that His Wrath crushes evil;
For this lies in evil's own nature.

The upward has the final word,
The downward cannot lastingly prevail.
O men, abandon foolishness, strive on —
Like eagles flying toward the sun.

Immortality

How canst thou call real what once was
And no longer is; the magic of destiny
That glided like a song over the lyre —
Time's play of strings; gone by, gone by.

Thou callest transient what in life's dream
Was once mortal, but then awoke to being:
The soul, that the Creator made eternal
Before it started journeying through time and space.

Blessèd is he whom Truth has kissed,
Who sees God's purpose in all things.
One loves the beautiful, because it tells of God;
One loves it, because it is profound and never dies.

Die Wahl

Du wählst den Weg der Wahrheit und des Seins,
Den du bei Shánkara und Plato findest:
Jenseits des Vielen ist das Große Eins.

Schau zu, dass du zum Selbst den Geist entzündest.
Dann magst du auch den Weg der Schönheit wählen —
Den Weg des Form gewordnen Wunderbaren.
Wer kann in süßer Nacht die Sterne zählen?

„Das Schöne ist der Strahlenkranz des Wahren."

Schauen

Der Edle sieht die Welt mit edlem Schauen;
Dem Reinen — sagt ein Spruch — ist alles rein.
Er sieht beim Wesen nicht zweideutgen Schein —
Nach Oben will er eine Brücke bauen.

Durchsichtig sind die Dinge für den Weisen;
Er will nicht bloß nach Außenformen fragen.
Er schaut die Botschaft, die sie in sich tragen —
Fühlt, wie sie Gott durch ihren Urklang preisen.

Der Edle sieht, was Gottes Absicht ist
In den Geschöpfen — sieht die Wesenstiefe,
Und nicht das Zufallsmäßige, das Schiefe;
Wohl dem, der mit des Himmels Maßen misst!

The Choice

Thou hast chosen the path of Truth and Being,
The path found in Plato and Shankara:
Beyond multiplicity is the Great One.

Take heed that thou inflame thy spirit for the Self.
Then thou may'st also choose the path of Beauty —
The path of the Wonderful become form.
Who can in sweet nights count the stars?

"The beautiful is the radiant garland of the True."

Seeing

The noble man looks at the world with noble gaze;
To the pure — it is said — all things are pure.
In the creature he sees not mere appearance —
He seeks to build a bridge on High.

Things are transparent for the sage;
He takes no interest in mere outward forms,
He looks at the message they carry within,
And feels how God is praised by their inner song.

The noble man sees what God's intention is
In creatures — he sees their deepest essence,
And not what is accidental and askew:
Blessèd is he who measures with Heaven's measures.

Paradoxon

Es ist nicht alles Gold, was glänzt; und dann:
Es glänzt nicht alles, was aus Gold sie machten.
Dies mag verwirren und enttäuschen, doch:
Man muss die Dinge ohne Wunsch betrachten.

Manchmal, o Mensch, sind Werte nur geliehen;
Und manche Werte bleiben ungesehen.
Befolge nicht Gefühls zu leichtes Spiel;
Verharre in der Wahrheit herben Höhen.

Der Dinge Wesen fasst des Adlers Blick;
Mit der Erscheinung sei geduldig, Seele.
Fürs Wahre ist des Menschen Herz gemacht;
So schaue zu, dass es das Wahre wähle.

Irrlehre

Sie sagen: liebet Gott und denket nicht;
Trinket die Seligkeit von Gottes Reben.
Ihr seht, woran es ihrem Geist gebricht:
Als wär das Denken nicht von Gott gegeben —

Als könnte man des Denkens Grenz nicht kennen,
Und dennoch Gottes Sein beim Namen nennen;
Als wär der Weise, der das Wort verehrt,
Nicht der vollkommnen Liebe Gottes wert!

Des Bhakta Seel: sie ist am Überschäumen
Und glüht — sie hat ihr eignes Recht aufs Träumen.

Paradoxon

Not everything is gold that glitters, and then:
Not everything glitters that is made of gold.
This may confuse and disappoint; however,
We ought to see things without wishful thought.

Sometimes, O man, qualities are merely borrowed;
And many qualities remain unseen.
Don't follow feeling's easy play,
But persevere in the stern heights of truth.

The eagle's eye perceives the essence of things;
Be patient then, O soul, with mere appearances.
The heart of man is destined for the true;
So take care that thy heart choose truth.

Heresy

They say: love God and do not think;
Just drink the wine of God's beatitude.
You see where their thinking falls short:
As if thought weren't a gift from God.

As if one could not know the limits of the mind,
And still call God's Being by name;
As if the sage who respects words,
Were unworthy of God's perfect love!

The *bhakta*'s soul is glowing
And exuberant — it has its own right to dream.

Die Antwort

Du sollst nicht fragen, was am Anfang war;
War es die Macht, der Geist, die Seligkeit?
Des Denkens und der Sprache Mittel sind
Nicht auf der Höhe der Unendlichkeit.

Des Denkens und der Sprache Kräfte können
Das Unaussprechliche nicht denkbar machen;
Sie geben Sinnbild, dunkel und doch wahr;
So können sie die Geistesschau entfachen.

Denn sieh: die Wahrheit, die du fassen möchtest,
Ist tief in deinen Geist hineingewoben;
Als Spiegel Gottes wurden wir gemacht;
Der Lichtstrahl ist das Licht. Gott lasst uns loben!

Menschsein

Menschsein ist schwer. Man kann nicht alles sein;
Man ist in Form und Schicksal eingeschlossen.
Dann kommt die Wahrheit, die der Traumwelt zürnt;
Gereinigt wird das Herz und umgegossen.

Du liebst die Erde, weil sie Mutter ist;
Nur eine Weile blüht der Heimat Flur.
Das Weltrad mag sich wie im Traume drehn —
Sprich: Gott!
　　　　　　Dann sei getrost und warte nur.

The Answer

Thou shouldst not ask what was in the beginning;
Was it Might, Spirit, or Beatitude?
The means of thought and speech are not
At the same level as Infinitude.

The powers of thought and speech cannot
Make the Inexpressible thinkable;
They give us symbols, obscure and yet true,
And thus they may kindle the Spirit's vision.

Behold: the truth that thou wishest to grasp
Is woven deeply into thine own spirit;
To be God's mirror we were made;
The ray of light is light itself. To God the praise!

To Be Man

To be man is difficult. One cannot be everything;
One is enclosed in form and destiny.
Then comes the Truth, opposing our dream-world;
The heart is purified and then recast.

Thou lovest Earth, because she is our mother;
But only for an instant does her meadow bloom.
The world-wheel turns as in a dream —
Say: God!
         Then simply trust and wait.

Das Wort

Inseln des Glücks, erblüht im fernsten Meer —
Ich weiß von keinem, der euch je gefunden.
Das Herz ist krank, die Sehnsucht lastet schwer
Mit Träumen, die sich um das Leere runden.

Dem Weisen ist der tiefe Sinn bekannt:
Er weiß von einem Wort, von Gott gegeben;
Nicht fernes Traumbild, sondern nahes Leben:
Der Höchste Name führt zu Allāhs Strand.

Einsicht

Wollt doch die Seel in ihrem Sein verharren!
Neid, Ehrgeiz, Eitelkeit und andre Laster
Entstellen sie; scheinheiliges Gemüt,
Vor allem Hochmut; nichts ist Gott verhasster.
Der Böse mag wohl viele Wunder wirken,
Sich hüllen in der Tugend schillernd Kleid;
Doch eines fehlt ihm, seine Maske fällt:
Zur wahren Demut ist er nie bereit.

Sei auf der Hut, o Mensch, und fürchte Gott;
Du kannst wohl glänzen, alle Welt belügen
Und dich bespiegeln in des Guten Schein;
Wach auf, du Tor; du kannst nicht Gott betrügen.
Im Menschen ist ein Riss, er kennt sich nicht.
O dass die Seel sich mit sich selbst versöhne!
Wahr ist die Gottheit, Wahrheit ist ihr Sein;
Und Sie ist schön; ihr Wesen liebt das Schöne.

Du Erdenmensch, du möchtest weise sein;
Verborgenes willst du bei Namen nennen.
Der Weisheit Anfang ist, dich selbst zu sehn —

Erkenne dich! Und du wirst Gott erkennen.

The Word

Islands of bliss, blossoming in distant seas —
I know of no one who has ever found you.
The heart is sick, nostalgia weighs it down
With dreams that gather round the void.

To the sage the deep meaning is known:
He knows a Word, given by God;
Not a distant dream, but closest life:
The Supreme Name leads us to Allah's shore.

Insight

Would the soul but rest in her own being!
Envy, ambition, vanity, and other vices
Disfigure her; she is filled with hypocrisy and
Above all pride; nothing is more hateful to God.
The Evil One may well work many wonders,
Enshroud himself in virtue's brilliant robe;
Yet one thing he lacks, his mask falls:
Never will he show true humility.

Be on guard, O man, and fear God,
Thou may'st well shine, and lie to the whole world,
And mirror thyself in the pretense of good;
Wake up, thou fool, thou canst not deceive God.
In man there is a fissure, he does not know himself.
O may the soul be reconciled with herself!
Divinity is true, Truth is its being
And It is beautiful; its Essence loveth Beauty.

O, earthly man, thou wishest to be wise;
To hidden things thou wishest to give names.
Wisdom's beginning is to see thyself —

Know thyself! And thou wilt know God.

Heiligkeit

Zwiefältig ist die Heiligkeit: die Eine
Stammt aus dem Willen, den die Lieb entzündet;
Die Andre ist Erkenntnis: wohl dem Geist,
Der Höchstes Gut durch tiefste Wahrheit findet.

Gewiss: des Frommen Krone ist Verdienst,
Aus seiner Heldenkraft herausgeboren.
Doch ebenso: die Krone ist Geschenk —

Der Selige ist göttlich auserkoren.

Ein Spruch

Wer Gott in seinem Seelengrund behütet,
Den wird auch Gott behüten in der Welt —
So sagt ein Spruch. Der Fürst des Bösen wütet;
An Gottes Mauer ist sein Zorn zerschellt.

Im Höchsten wohne; Er wird in dir wohnen.
Was willst du mehr? Du kannst das Rad nicht halten,
Die Zeit zerrinnt. Der Herr wird dich belohnen
Für die Geduld.
        So lass den Höchsten walten.

Die Werte

Zuerst die Wahrheit, die die Seele rettet;
Und dann das stete Denken an das Wahre.
Sodann der Seele Adel: eingebettet
In Schönheit seien deines Weges Jahre.

Dies sind die hohen Werte, die dein Geist
Stets im Bewusstsein tragen soll; das Andre
Ist in des Höchsten Hand. Und was du weißt,
Beherzige! Vertrau auf Gott und wandre.

Sanctity

Twofold is sanctity: one kind
Stems from the will, kindled by love;
The other is knowledge: blest be the mind
Who finds the Highest Good through deepest Truth.

Indeed the crown of pious men is merit,
It is born of heroic strength.
But even so: the crown is a gift —

The blessèd one is chosen by the Lord.

A Saying

Whoso protects God in the depth of his soul,
Him will God protect in the world —
Thus it is said. The Prince of Darkness rages;
His anger is shattered against the Wall of God.

Abide in the Most High; He will abide in thee.
What more dost thou wish? Thou canst not halt the wheel,
Time melts away. The Lord will reward thee
For thy patience.
                    So let the Most High reign.

Values

First the Truth, that saves the soul;
Then ceaseless thinking on the True.
Then our nobility of soul: arrayed
In beauty be the path of thy years.

These are the highest values which thy mind
Should always carry in its consciousness.
The rest is in the Hands of God. And what thou knowest,
Take to heart! Trust in God, and journey on.

Das Leben

Du wähnst, da sei ein Leben, doch bedenke
Dass in der Tat der Leben viele sind.
Die Zeit verwandelt: warst du nicht ein Kind?
Du wirst ein Greis; dann schließt des Lebens Schenke.

Dann öffnet sich das Tor der andren Welt.
Ist denn ein Erdenleben je gewesen?
Von allem Traumtrug bist du jäh genesen:
Das Wahre leuchtet, und der Wahn zerfällt.

Dein Kern birgt mehr als Lebens kurze Frist;
Gott mag dich leiten — bis du ewig bist.

Das Sein

Was ist des höchsten Seins verborgner Sinn?
Das Seiende wird sein, ist stets gewesen?
Ihr habt es in der Heilgen Schrift gelesen:
Das Eine ist. Sein Name ist: Ich bin.

Der Dornbusch brannte, doch verbrannte nicht;
Das Brennen war nicht Feuer, sondern Licht
Aus Gottes Sein. Kein Leuchten, das man misst,
Doch Zeichen, Wunderkraft —
                              von Dem, der ist.

Life

Thou art deceived in thinking: there is one life;
Think rather that in fact our lives are many.
Time transforms: wast thou not a child?
Soon thou wilt be old, and the tavern of life will close.

Then the door to the next world will open.
Was there ever a life on earth?
Of all dream-deceit thou art suddenly cured:
The True shines forth and illusion shatters.

Thy kernel holds more than life's short term;
May God lead thee — till thou art eternal.

Being

What is the hidden meaning of the Highest Being?
That which is, will be, and has always been?
You have read it in the Scriptures:
The One is. And Its Name is: I AM.

The thorn-bush burned, yet it was not consumed;
The burning was not fire, but light
From God's Being. A light not to be measured
But a sign, a miraculous power —
                                        of Him who is.

Sinceritas

Der Mensch vor Gott und Welt: dies ist die Frage,
Die alle andern Fragen in sich fasst.
Bist du mit Gott in Frieden, wohl, so trage
Der Welt Verkehrtheit und der Seele Last.

Frag mich, was Menschen wert sind, und ich frage
Was ihr Verhalten vor dem Höchsten Gut.
Jedwelches Schicksal hat wohl seine Plage —
Glückselig, wer im Willen Gottes ruht.

Freude

Dies musst du lernen: dich am Höchsten Gut
   Restlos zu freuen,
Und von des Lebens ärgerlichem Kram
   Nichts zu bereuen.

Du musst es lernen: kindlich dankbar sein
   Im Angesichte
Des Höchsten; denn das Gottgedenken macht
   Den Kram zunichte.

O Freude, von der Gnade Strahl geschenkt,
   Du bist der Morgen,
In dem die Seele neu geboren wird —
   Bei Gott geborgen.

Sinceritas

Man before God and world: this is the question
That contains all other questions.
If with God thou hast found thy peace, then thou canst bear
The world's absurdities, and burdens of thy soul.

Ask me what men are worth and I will ask
What their comportment is before the Sovereign Good.
Each destiny may have its troubles —
Blessèd the man reposing in God's Will.

Joy

This must thou learn: wholly to rejoice
        In the Sovereign Good,
And to regret nothing
        Of life's vexatious din.

Thou must learn: to be thankful like a child
        In the face of the Most High;
For the remembrance of God reduces
        Worldly things to naught.

O Joy, bestowed by the ray of Grace,
        Thou art the morning
In which the soul is born anew —
        Sheltered in God.

Welträtsel

Sagt nicht, der ganze Kosmos sei nur Staub
Und weiter nichts. Dies könnte schwer betrüben;
Was bliebe übrig? Kann man denn die Welt
In ihrer Ganzheit in das Nichts verschieben?

Ihr sagt, sie sei bloß Trug und nichtger Tand.
Gebt acht: die Welt verkündet Höchstes Gut;
In jedem Sandkorn tut das Sein sich kund.
Klein und vergänglich? Göttlich ist der Sand.

So sollt ihr auch die kleinsten Dinge achten:
Das Daseinswunder, nicht des Daseins Mängel;
Und dann der Dinge Gutes, das sie adelt.
In jedem Sandkorn wirkt des Werdens Engel.

Pfade

Das Leere nur bringt uns zum Geist, zum Heile:
Dies ist die enge Gasse des Verzichts.
Das Unsichtbare lieben, auch das Schöne:
Dies ist der edle Pfad des Gleichgewichts.

Und dieser Pfad erfordert einen Blick
Der durch die Formen bis zum Urbild dringt.
Des Herzens Auge schaut das wahre Sein,
Wo Höchsten Gutes Harmonie erklingt.

In edler Menschen Liebe liegt Verzicht:
Man darf das Schöne nicht aus Lust berauben.
Und andrerseits: der Büßer, der verwirft,
Muss an die Schönheit heilger Dinge glauben.

Zwiespältigkeit — sie soll dich nicht betrüben;
Das Liebenswerte darf der Edle lieben.
Ihr möget blind sein, dies ist kein Vergehen —
Der Weise wird das Licht im Dunklen sehen.

World-enigma

Say not the Cosmos is but dust
And nothing more. For this could make you sad;
What would remain? Can one then drive the world
In its entirety into nothingness?

You say it is illusion, idle play.
Take heed: the world is harbinger of Highest Good.
In every grain of sand Being is manifest.
Fleeting and small? The sand is divine.

You should respect even the smallest things:
The wonder of Existence, not its flaws;
And then the good in things, that ennobles them.
In every grain of sand the Angel of becoming acts.

Paths

The Void alone leads to the Spirit, to salvation:
This is the narrow way of renunciation.
Love of the unseen and the beautiful:
This is the noble path of equilibrium.

The second path demands a vision
That through forms pierces to the archetype.
The heart's eye perceives true Being,
Where the music of the Highest Good resounds.

In noble love there lies renunciation:
One must not rob the beautiful through lust.
But on the other hand, the penitent, renouncing,
Must believe in the beauty of all sacred things.

Divergence — let it not trouble thee;
The noble man may love what is worthy of love.
Ye may be blind, this is no sin —
The sage, in the darkness, will see light.

Vom Schönen

Die Wahrheit liebt der Schönheit edlen Kranz.
Beweis: des Schönen Dasein. Wär nichts wert
Geliebt zu werden, gäb es keine Liebe.
Und dann: man liebt nicht, was man nicht verehrt.

Eifer muss mild sein, wie die reinste Quelle;
Ein Heilger sprach: das Bittre führt zur Hölle.
Verwerfung eitler Lust ist recht; allein
Der Weg zum Höchsten kann nicht hässlich sein.

Der Weg zum Himmel kennt nicht Eigensucht
Noch Ehrgeiz; er ist edles Selbstvergessen.
Schaut, was die allerhöchsten Werte sind —
Denn was ihr wert seid, könnt ihr nicht ermessen.

Berufung

Schönheit erfordert Tugend, weil sie sonst
Entweihung ist, eitle Narzissus-Sünde;
Gott will nicht, dass das schöne Weib sich stolz
Den Kranz des Sieges um die Schläfen winde.

Und so des Menschen Geist: er wirket nicht
Um Eitles auszubrüten, zum Verderben;
Berufung ist, das gottgegebne Licht
Zu säen und das Himmelreich zu erben —

Denn Gottes Gabe ist des Menschen Pflicht.

Of the Beautiful

Truth loves the noble wreath of beauty.
Proof: the beautiful exists. Were there
Nothing worthy of love, love would not even be.
And then: one cannot love what one does not revere.

Zeal must be gentle, like the purest spring;
A saint has said: bitterness leads to hell.
Idle pleasures it is right to leave behind,
But the path to God cannot be ugly.

The path to Heaven knows no selfishness
And no ambition; it is a noble self-forgetfulness.
See what the highest values are —
You cannot measure what your worth may be.

Vocation

All beauty demands virtue, otherwise
It is a profanation, the vain sin of Narcissus;
God does not wish the beautiful woman
To proudly wind the wreath of victory about her brow.

Likewise the human mind: it is not meant
To hatch vain things, to spoil or to destroy;
Our vocation is to sow the light given by God
And to inherit the Kingdom of Heaven.

For God's gift is man's obligation.

Seele

Man sagt, dass Liebe alles Werden schaffe,
Sie sei die Triebkraft, die die Welt bewege;
Erkenntnis sei des Ewgen Wesens Kern,
Dass alles sinngemäß gelingen möge.

Und so die Seele: unterscheide wohl
Was Sein ist und was Schein. Die Liebe wirkt
Das edle Leben hin zu Gott und Welt —
Auf dass erstrahle, was die Weisheit birgt.

Nach Salomo

Des Weisen Geist wohnt in Besinnungs Klause;
Nicht so der Tor, der freudig schwelgt beim Schmause
Und an nichts denkt. Was ist das End vom Liede?
Ihm fehlt das Wesentliche — Gottes Friede,
Der über allem Erdentaumel thront
Und in des Weisen Herzenstiefe wohnt.

Das Herz des Weisen ist im Trauerhause,
Sagt Salomo; der Narr ist in der Freude,
Er lebt von Tag zu Tag, ihn kümmert nichts,
Hart ist das Herz des eitlen Bösewichts —
Der Weise weiß von dieses Daseins Leide.

Mag doch der Narr verspotten und verprassen —
Das Weltrad dreht sich, wie der Himmel will,
Und eines fernen Tages steht es still —

Gott wird die weise Seele nicht verlassen.

Soul

They say that love gives rise to all becoming,
That it is the driving force that moves the world;
That knowledge is the kernel of Eternal Being,
So everything may prosper according to its due.

Likewise the soul: discern well
What Being is, and what appearance;
Loves inspires noble life toward God and the world —
So all that wisdom contains may be brought to light.

According to Solomon

The wise mind dwells in the retreat of meditation;
Not so the unwise, who blithely revels in feasting
And thinks of nothing. What is the story's end?
He lacks what is essential — the Peace of God
Enthroned on high above the frenzy of the world,
And dwelling deep in the wise man's heart.

The wise man's heart is in the house of mourning,
Says Solomon; that of the fool is in enjoyment;
Living from day to day, nothing concerns him.
Hard is the heart of the vain evil-doer —
The wise man knows the suffering of existence.

Let the fool mock, let him be prodigal —
The world-wheel turns as Heaven wills,
And in a day far off it will come to a halt —

Never will God abandon the wise soul.

Ein Psalm

Der König David sang: Gott ist mein Heil,
Mir wird nichts mangeln; denn der Herr ist hier.
Ob ich auch wanderte im finstern Tal
Des Todes, fürcht ich nichts; Er ist bei mir.

Bedenket, Menschen, dass Er gütig ist
Dem, der auf seine Gnade voll vertraut
Und sein Gesetz liebt, und vor Liebe tanzt –
Des Seele ist des Allerhöchsten Braut.

Zurück

Aufsteigend ist der Weg, ins höchste Leere;
Dann aber, heißt es, käme uns ein Ruf:
Zurück zur Welt, mit einer Himmelsgabe;
Ein Gnadenwunder, das der Höchste schuf.

Der Geistespfad ist wie ein Regenbogen:
Man steigt zum Licht empor, dann kehrt man wieder;
Man sieht Gott in der Welt, die Welt in Ihm.
Von dieser Rückkehr zeugen unsre Lieder.

Jetzt

Ewiges Jetzt des Gottgedenkens: seht
Wie für das Menschenkind die Zeit vergeht.

Im Geistesleben gibt es keine Zeit:
Nur Jetzt im Göttlichen, nur Ewigkeit.

Der Außenmensch erlebt des Daseins Fülle;
Der Innenmensch verharrt in Gottes Stille.

Der Weg: was ist das letzte Wort vom Liede?
Der Sang des Paradieses: Friede, Friede.

A Psalm

King David sang: The Lord is my salvation;
I shall not want, for He is here.
And though I walk through the dark valley
Of death, I do not fear, for He is with me.

O man, remember He is gracious
To him who in His Mercy fully trusts,
And loves His Law, and dances out of love —
Whose soul is bride unto the Lord Most High.

Returning

The path goes upward to the Highest Void;
But then, it is said, a call will come to us:
Return with Heaven's gift into the world;
A miracle of grace, created by the Most High.

And like a rainbow is the Spirit's path:
One rises to the light, and then returns again;
One sees God in the world, and then the world in Him.
To this return our songs bear witness.

Now

Eternal Now of God-remembrance:
See how for man time passes by.

In spiritual life there is no time:
Only the Now in the Divine, only Eternity.

The outer man experiences the fullness of existence;
The inner man reposes in God's stillness.

The Path: what is the last word of the song?
The melody of Paradise: Peace, Peace.

Scheich Achmed

Was ist der Glaube, was ist frommes Tun?
Der Schriftgelehrsamkeit gestrenge Noten —
Der Streit darüber, was recht, was verboten?
Im Großen Einen soll die Seele ruhn.

Scheich Achmed sprach: Der Offenbarung Gut
Ist in der Gottheit Namen voll enthalten;
In ihm sind der Barmherzigkeit Gewalten —
Glückselig, wer in Allāhs Namen ruht.

Islām

Alles auf Erden wird dereinst vergehen;
Es heißet: Lā ilāha illā 'Llāh —
Daher Vergänglichkeit, lehrt der Koran.
Wer kann vor Allāh's Angesicht bestehen?

Doch: wenn du wüsstest, dass das Weltgericht
Für morgen wär — du tätest deine Pflicht,
Als hättest du noch hundert Jahr zu leben.
Sei ruhig, Herz — lass Gott dein Schicksal weben.

Shaikh Ahmad

What is faith, what is pious conduct?
The stern qualities of scholarship —
Disputing what is lawful, and what is not?
In the Great One the soul should rest.

Shaikh Ahmad said: the wealth of Revelation
Is fully contained in the Name of God;
In it are all the powers of Mercy —
Blessed is he who rests in Allah's Name.

Islam

One day all things on earth will be no more;
It is said: *Lā ilāha illā 'Llāh* —
Hence transience, teaches the Koran.
Who can go on existing before the Face of Allah?

Yet, if thou didst know the Last Judgment
Were tomorrow — thou wouldst thy duties still perform
As if another hundred years thou hadst to live.
O heart, be still, and let God weave thy destiny.

Rätselspiel

Allmöglichkeit: wer kann ihr widerstehn?
Ihr fragt: warum erlaubt denn Gott das Schlechte?
Warum nicht nur das Gute, das Gerechte?
Wer kann der Schöpfung Rätselspiel verstehn?

Das Nichts verfolgt das Dasein wie ein Schatten,
Will es verwunden, kann es nie besiegen.
Das Nichts kann nie im wahren Wesen liegen —
Mag auch des Daseins Blütenbaum ermatten.

Gott wollte sich in tausend Spiegeln sehen,
Die Seelen, die des Schicksals Aug erspäht.
Hat eines Tags der Tod sie weggemäht —
Das Sein belebt sie, dass sie auferstehen.

Allmöglichkeit: Ursein hat keinen Rand
Der Es begrenzt; Es will das Weltall weben;
So lässt Es selbst das Nichts zum Scheine leben —
Sei still, mein Herz.
                    Du bist in Gottes Hand.

Alter

Im Alter muss man ganz sich selber werden
Und dennoch anders: war die Kindheit recht,
So bleib ihr treu; war manches Äußre schlecht,
So muss es schwinden. Was ist gut auf Erden?

Wenn du vor Gott stehst, jetzt, zu dieser Zeit:
Du warst nie aus dem Stoff, der Gott vergisst.
So werde, was du warst, nein, was du bist —

Und sei zur ewgen Gottesschau bereit.

Play of Riddles

All-Possibility: who can withstand it?
You ask: why, then, does God permit evil?
Why not only the good, and the just?
Who can understand creation's play of riddles?

The naught pursues Existence like a shadow,
It seeks to wound it, but can never win.
Nothingness cannot lie in the essence of things,
Though the flowering tree of Existence should fade.

In countless mirrors God wished to see Himself:
The souls that the eye of destiny espies.
When one day death has taken them away —
Being will revive them, they will be resurrected.

All-Possibility: the Divine Essence is boundless,
Without limit. It wills to weave the Universe,
So It lets even nothingness pretend to be.
Be still, my heart.
                    Thou art in God's Hands.

Age

In old age one must become entirely oneself;
Yet also different: if thy childhood was good,
Remain faithful to it; if outwardly there was much bad,
Then it must disappear. What is there good on earth?

When thou standest before thy God, now, at this time:
Thy substance was never such that would forget God.
Thus become what thou wast, nay, what thou art —

And be prepared for the eternal vision of God.

Innerlichkeit

Inwendig in der Seel ist Gottes Reich;
Und wenn ihr betet, schließt das Kämmerlein;
Und betet ohne Unterlass, im Geist;
Nicht Menschensatzung soll Gesetz euch sein;
Dies ist es, was der Nazarener sprach.

Ich schlafe, doch mein Herz, mein Herz ist wach!

Beten

Ist das Gebet nicht überall, enthalten
    In allen Dingen?
Du hörst den Wind, den Wald, den Strom, das Meer
    Vom Höchsten singen.

Ihr sollet beten ohne Unterlass —
    Dies steht geschrieben;
Ihr sollet Gott in allem, was ihr tut,
    Von Herzen lieben.

Alles in Einem

Wir halten uns an Eins: an Gottes Namen —
Er ist für unsre Gottesschau der Rahmen.
Er gibt Gewissheit: Gott ist wirklich da;
Wir rufen Ihn, erwachen — sind Ihm nah!

Im Namen ist die ganze Lehr verborgen,
Auch Gottes Wille, Seelen zu erlösen;
Die Seele will von dieser Welt genesen,
So ist denn unser Ruf ein Frühlingsmorgen —

O leuchte, Höchstes Licht, zu meinem Liede!
Der Name und mein Herz: Gott und der Friede.

Inwardness

God's kingdom is within the soul;
So when ye pray, shut well your chamber door;
And pray in spirit, without ceasing;
The rules of men should not be law to you;
This is what the Nazarene has taught.

I sleep, but my heart, my heart is awake!

Prayer

Is prayer not everywhere contained
        In every thing?
Thou hearest the wind, the woods, the river, and the sea
        Sing of the Most High.

Ye should pray without ceasing —
        Thus was it written;
Ye should, in everything ye do, love God
        With all your heart.

All in One

We hold fast to one thing: to God's Name —
It is the frame for our vision of God.
It gives us certitude that God is really here;
We call Him, we awake — and we are near to Him.

All sacred teaching is hidden within the Name,
So is the Divine Will to save our souls;
The soul wants to be cured of this poor world,
And so like a spring morning is our call —

O highest Light, shine down upon my song!
The Name and my heart: God and Peace.

Pax

Der Weise hat in sich die Welt besiegt,
Die uns befeindet, uns das Herz zerreißt;
Er ist der Adler, der zur Sonne fliegt —
So steigt der Pfeife Rauch zum Großen Geist.

Wohlan, der Gottesmann muss Krieger sein;
Dies will die Welt, die dauernd uns betört.
Doch dann: was ist der Heilgen Pfeife Sinn?

Der Friede, dem des Weisen Herz gehört.

Das Eine

Bedenke, Mensch, du kannst es nicht vermeiden:
Du wirst, o Seele, vor dem Einen stehen,
Das deiner harret; früher oder spät
Wirst du nicht Vielheit, nur das Eine sehen.

Doch dieses Eine ist nicht Armut, Mangel,
Es ist das Alles, ist die Himmelspfort —
Ja Gottes Fülle, die das Dasein zeugt
Und neu belebt —
                    Am Anfang war das Wort.

Pax

The sage has conquered the world within himself,
The world, which is our enemy and rends the heart;
The sage is like an eagle flying to the sun —
Thus the Pipe's smoke to the Great Spirit rises.

Indeed, the man of God must be a warrior;
The world, which ever dazzles us, makes this demand.
But then: what is the meaning of the Sacred Pipe?

The Peace to which the wise man's heart belongs.

The One

O man, consider that which thou canst not avoid:
Thou wilt, O soul arrive before the One —
It waits for thee; sooner or later
Thou wilt see, not the many, but the One.

Yet this One is neither poverty nor want,
It is the All, the gate of Paradise —
The fullness of God, which begets existence
And gives it life anew —
                    In the beginning was the Word.

Doppelleben

Ihr wisst nicht, was es ist, das Doppelleben
Des Weisen, der zwei Welten muss vereinen:
Die Innere, die ihn zum Höchsten zieht;
Die Äußere, — er kann sie nicht verneinen,

Und will es nicht, da Gott sie schöpfen wollte.
Ist nicht ihr Traumstoff Blut von unserm Blute?
Zwiespältig ist das All, und dennoch eins —

Denn alles Edle zeugt vom Höchsten Gute.

Samsāra

Der Mensch ist höchste Lebensform auf Erden:
Ein edles menschliches Geschöpf zu werden —
So lehrt der Osten — ist ein seltnes Glück;
Menschsein ist Ganzheit, Tiersein ist nur Stück.
Der Menschenzustand ist das Tor zum Heil —
Nicht ohne Mühe, denn der Pfad ist steil.

So irren sie in dieser Leidenswelt
Wo alles stirbt, vergeht, verwelkt, zerfällt.
Der Buddha wünscht, dass alle glücklich seien:
Ihm steht es zu, die Botschaft auszustreuen.
Er tut es nicht mit seinem Wort allein —

Es strahlt im Finstern sein erhabnes Sein.

Double Life

You do not know what makes the double life
Of the sage, who must unite two worlds:
The inner one, which draws him toward the Highest;
The outer one, which he cannot deny,

And neither does he wish to, since God created it.
Is not its dream-stuff blood of our blood?
The universe is fragmented, yet it is one —

All that is noble speaks of the Sovereign Good.

Samsara

Man is the highest form of life on earth:
To become a noble human being
Is rare fortune — this is the teaching of the East;
To be a man is wholeness, to be an animal mere part.
The human state is gate to salvation —
But not without effort, for the path is steep.

And so man roams this world of suffering,
Where everything is dying, passing, fading, crumbling.
The Buddha wishes that all should be happy:
His duty is to spread the message far and wide.
He does not do this with his word alone —

His serene being shines into the dark.

Der Beweis

Was ist denn der Beweis — hat man gefragt —
Dass es ein Paradies gibt? Sieh die Pracht
Der Blumen, Blüten; wär kein Paradies,
So hätte Gott die Schönheit nicht gemacht!

Dies ist nicht bloße Meinung, es ist Sehen —
Die Dinge selbst sind unfehlbares Denken.
Ich bin in ihnen, und sie sind in mir;
Sie sind es, die mir ihre Wahrheit schenken.

Ihr mögt verstehen oder nicht verstehen —
Im Zeichen kann das Herz den Urgrund sehen.

Yin-Yang

Ein schwarzer Punkt in einem weißen Feld,
Und umgekehrt: ein weißer Punkt im Dunkeln.
In diesem Wechsel liegt die ganze Welt;
Sieh wie der Formen viele Seiten funkeln.

Erkenne wohl das Wechselspiel der Dinge:
In jedem findest du etwas vom andern.
Du magst das grenzenlose All durchwandern:
Die Wahrheit liegt auf einer scharfen Klinge.

Darüber strahlt das Tao, höchstes Licht —
Ganz ohne Gegensatz, das Große Eine.
Du willst es fassen, es gelingt dir nicht —

O dass die Weisheit Tag und Nacht vereine:
Wort und Geheimnis. Bleibe, was du bist —
Im Einen wirst du schauen: Das, was ist.

The Proof

It has been asked — what is the proof
That there is Paradise? Look at the splendor
Of blossoms and flowers: were there no Paradise,
God would not have made beauty!

This is no mere opinion: it is vision —
Things themselves are infallible thought.
I am in them and they are in me;
It is they who bestow on me their truth.

You may understand, or not understand —
The heart can see the Essence in outward signs.

Yin-Yang

A black dot in a white field,
And the converse: a white dot in the dark.
The whole world lies in this exchange;
See how the many facets of forms are sparkling.

And recognize the interplay of things:
In each you find something of the other.
Well may you wander through the boundless All:
The Truth lies on a blade's edge.

Above it shines the Tao, sublime light —
Wholly without opposite, the Great One.
You wish to grasp it, but do not succeed —

O that wisdom may unite day and night:
Word and mystery. Remain what you are —
In the One you will see That which is.

Die Moiren

Klotho, die unsern Lebensfaden spinnt;
Dann Láchesis, die ihn uns zuerteilt;
Und Atropos, die ihn durchschneiden muss.
Und keiner, den das Schicksal nicht ereilt.

Du bist unsterblich. Habe Zuversicht:
Der Moiren Spiel berührt dein Herze nicht.

Gnosis

Der offenbarte Glaube spricht zu allen;
Geheim, weil schwierig, ist der Weisheitskern.
Die Gnosis ist nicht Form, sie ist nicht Zeit;
Den Weisen leitet ein verborgner Stern.

In einem Sinne ist die Gnosis Teil
Des Glaubens, feingesponnener Gehalt;
Doch andrerseits bleibt ihre Tiefe fremd
Dem Joche pharisäischer Gewalt.

Wer kann der Gottesweisen Wort begreifen?
Ich bin nicht Jude, nicht Moslem, nicht Christ,
So sagte Rumi; mein Islam ist nicht
Geformter Glaube; er ist das, was ist.

O Herzenslicht, das vor dem Höchsten steht,
Das immer war, das nimmermehr vergeht.

The Fates

Clotho, who spins the thread of our life,
Then Lachesis, who apportions it to us,
And Atropos, who must cut through it.
There is no one whom destiny does not overtake.

Thou art immortal. Be thou confident:
The play of Fates never touches the heart.

Gnosis

Revealed faith speaks to every man;
Secret and difficult is the kernel of wisdom.
Gnosis is not form, nor is it time;
The sage is guided by a hidden star.

In one sense gnosis is a part
Of faith, its content finely spun;
And yet the depth of gnosis still remains
Beyond the yoke of pharisaic power.

Who can fathom the word of God's wise men?
I am neither a Jew, nor Muslim, nor Christian,
Rumi said; and my Islam is not
Dogmatic belief; it is that which is.

O light of the heart, shining before the Most High,
Which always was and nevermore shall fade.

Homo sapiens

Es ist doch seltsam, dass der Erdenmensch
Das Grenzenlose niemals kann erfassen;
Sein Lebensdrang, sein tastender Verstand,
Bewegt sich in des Daseins engen Gassen.

Jedoch: der reine Geist, das tiefe Herz,
Erfasst das überweltlich Schrankenlose;
Der Geist ist unerschaffen, ist nicht ich —
Der Außenmensch sei froh mit seinem Lose.

Du magst nach Innen schauen, in die Tiefe —
Et hoc est Intellectus. Es genügt
Mitnichten. Denn die Gottheit ist an Sich —
Bevor du warst. Du bist's, die in Ihr liegt.

Mensch, Gottesspiegel. Sag, was ist dein Sinn?
Gott wollte sich im Sein des Nichts erkennen.
Erkennst du Gott? Er ist's, der Sich erkennt
In dir.
        Dein Geist ist nicht von Gott getrennt.

Homo Sapiens

How strange: the mind of earthly man
Can never grasp the limitless;
His love of life, his uncertain understanding,
Move in the narrow byways of existence.

And yet the Spirit, the deep heart,
May grasp the metacosmic Limitless;
The Spirit is uncreated, it is not I —
Let the outer man be happy with his modest destiny!

Inward thou mayest look, into thy depth —
Et hoc est Intellectus. But this is not
Enough. For the Godhead is self-existent —
Before thou wert. 'Tis thou, who art contained in It.

O man, mirror of God. Tell me: what is thy meaning?
God wished to see Himself in nothingness.
Dost thou know God? He is the one who sees Himself
In thee.
                Thy spirit is not separate from God.

Vom Bösen

Das sollt ihr nicht vergessen: es ist klar
Dass Übles immer in euch selber war;
Jedoch des bösen Spielverderbers List
Kommt noch dazu — und schlimmer, als ihr wisst.

Ihr kennet ja der Seele heilgen Krieg
Wider sich selbst; ihr wisst von Geistes Sieg.
Hört nicht auf das, was euch der Böse sagt;
Gleichgültig seid, wenn euch sein Lügen plagt.

Er wird euch sagen, ihr seid wunderbar.
Gleichgültig ist, ob's falsch ist oder wahr.
Er wird euch sagen, ihr seid hilflos böse;
Dies kann kaum sein.
                            Dass uns doch Gott erlöse!

Die Höchsten

Wer ist der Heilige, wer ist der Weise,
Wer der Prophet, des Herz in Liebe brennt?
Was sind die gotterfüllten Menschen — Höhen,
Die unsre Zeit nicht kennen will, nicht kennt?

Die Höchsten blähn sich nicht; sie wollen nicht
Besitzer ihrer Tugend sein; sie stehen
Vor Gott, empfangend, was der Geist verschenkt —

Sie lassen Gott durch ihre Seele gehen.

Evil

This you should not forget: it is clear that
Some evil always was in you.
The wicked malefactor's ruse
Then adds to it — and more so than you know.

You know of course the Holy War
Against oneself; you know the Spirit's victory.
So do not listen to the Evil One,
And be indifferent to his tormenting lies.

He will tell you that you are wonderful.
True or false, this is indifferent.
He will tell you that you are hopelessly bad;
This is improbable.
                    And may God save us all!

The Highest Ones

Who is the saint, and who the sage,
Who is the prophet whose heart burns with love?
What are the people filled with God — heights
Our time knows not, nor wants to know?

The highest ones are not puffed up, they do not seek
To own their virtues; they stand
Before God and receive the Spirit's gifts —

They let God permeate their souls.

Amida

Warum ist Amitābhas Paradies
Im kühlen Westen, wo die Sonne sinkt?
Warum in jener Ferne, wo die Nacht
Den letzten Kelch des goldnen Tages trinkt?

Der Sinn: das Ende aller Leidenschaft —
Der Ort, wo alle Selbstsucht uns verließ.
Amidas Name kennt nicht Dunkelheit —
In lichtem Gold erstrahlt sein Paradies.

Handeln, Erkennen

Verschieden sind die Regeln, weil der Menschen
Gar viele sind — verschieden ist ihr Denken
Und Fühlen. Die Gesetze müssen sein,
Gewiss — um Menschen auf dem Weg zu lenken.

Der Gläubige, der nur der Regel traut,
Besitzet nicht der Weisheit letzten Schluss;
Er hält für einzig gut was tun er muss;
Der Weise auf der Dinge Wesen schaut.

Verachte nicht des Glaubenskindes Streben;
Doch lass den Weisen in der Wahrheit leben.
Handeln befreit vom Irren nicht —
                              Erkennen
Allein kann allen Erdentrug verbrennen.

Amida

Why is the Paradise of Amitabha
In the cool West, where the sun goes down?
Why in that distant place, wherein the night
Drinks the last cup of golden day?

The meaning is: it is where passion ends —
The place where every selfish thought has left us.
Amida's Name no darkness knows —
His Paradise is shining in bright gold

To Act, to Know

Rules are diverse, because there are so many men —
Their thinking and their feelings are diverse.
Clearly, laws must be —
To guide men on the Path.

Believers who rely on rules alone
Do not possess the final word of wisdom.
They deem good only that which they must do;
The sage alone sees the essence of things.

Do not despise the efforts of the child of faith,
But let the wise man live within the Truth.
Action does not liberate from error —
                                    Knowledge
Alone consumes the world's deceit.

Zeichen

Vorzeichen gibt es. Doch der Böse will
Euch überzeugen, alles sei ein Zeichen
Und nimmt euch alle Ruh. Geduld, Geduld,
Und Mut! Ihr dürft nicht von der Stelle weichen —

Denn alles ist in Gottes Hand. Ihr könnt
Die Welt nicht ändern. Doch ihr könnt und sollt
Auf Gott vertraun. So nehmt in Ruhe an
Was euch verbessert —
                                        Und was Gott gewollt.

Die Helle

Im hohen Alter weiß man, dass das Leben
Ein Nebelschleier ist, den Feen weben;
Man frägt sich, was die Welt ist — und dabei
Weiß man es allzu gut; man zählt auf drei.

Und hinter dem Gewebe ist die Helle,
Die Friede schenkt und deren Trost man trinkt —
Ein lichter Strom, des wundersame Welle
Uns an den goldnen Strand der Gottheit bringt.

Omens

Omens exist. But the Evil One
Wants to convince you they are everywhere
And takes away your peace. Patience, patience,
And courage! Don't yield an inch —

For everything is in God's Hands. You cannot
Change the world. But you can, and must,
Have trust in God. So tranquilly accept
What makes you better —
                                    And what God has willed.

Clarity

In ripe old age one knows that life
Is but a veil of mist that fairies weave;
One wonders what the world is — and one knows
All too well; no more is one naïve.

Behind this fabric is the clarity
That bestows peace and whose solace one drinks —
A river of light, whose wondrous wave
Transports us to the golden shore of God.

Die Dauer

Dauer zermürbt die Seel der meisten Menschen.
Den Weisen mahlet nicht die Mühle Zeit:
Er steht vor Gott, frägt nicht nach Wann und Wo,
Stets zu des Herzens Tiefenschau bereit.

Des Toren Herz verdorrt im Gottvergessen,
Sein Leben altert und die Welt wird kalt —
Der Tor kann nicht des Daseins Traumspiel messen.

Ewiges Jetzt — der Weise wird nicht alt.
Gewiss, er muss den Lauf des Lebens kosten
In allen kleinen Dingen, die geschehen;
Jedoch des Geistes Wurzel ist in Gott —
Das Zeitrad mag sich endlos weiter drehen.

Mahnwort

Der Mensch muss wählen: soll das Herz ihm brechen?
Soll er, wie Jesus, auf dem Wasser gehn,
Ein Sieger? Es gibt keine andre Wahl
Wenn uns des Schicksals bittre Dornen stechen.

Deshalb: steh auf dem Felsen. Schau empor
Und bleib im Frieden; alles geht vorbei,
Nur nicht das Höchste Gut, das dich befreit —
Das deiner harrt. Der Rest ist einerlei.

Duration

Duration wears down the souls of many men,
But the mill of time does not grind down the sage;
Standing before God, not asking where or when,
He is always ready for the deep vision of the heart.

Oblivious of God, the fool's heart withers,
His life grows old, the world grows cold —
The fool cannot measure the dream-play of existence.

Eternal Now — the wise man ages not.
Clearly, he must taste the stream of life
In all the little things that happen;
And yet his Spirit stays rooted in God —
Let the world-wheel without ceasing turn round.

Admonition

Man has to choose: should his heart break?
Should he, like Jesus, walk upon the waters,
A victor? There is no other choice
When we are stung by bitter thorns of fate.

Therefore: stand fast upon a rock. Look upward
And remain in peace; all things will pass,
All save the Sovereign Good that liberates
And waits for thee. The rest is indifferent.

Gegenwart

Das Jetzt vor Gott; ich sag es tausendmal.
Kein Vorher und kein Nachher; nur der Strahl
Des Höchsten Namens, der das Herz erfüllt
Und dessen allertiefste Sehnsucht stillt.

Dies ist das Gottgedenken. Doch das Tun
Des Tags geht weiter, und wir müssen's wagen.
Lass Gott die Bürde deines Alltags tragen —
In seinem Namen kannst du immer ruhn.

Die Lehre

Das Lehrgebäude ist ein heilig Haus;
Ihr könnt nicht auf der Lehre Wort verzichten
Und wähnen, alles sei im Gottesrausch;
Dies hieße ja, der Wahrheit Form vernichten.

Am Anfang war das Wort; neigt euch zur Erd;
Dann kommt der Weg: halb Kampf, halb Herzensglück;
Die Tugend dann, des Seelenadels Duft —
Dreifältig ist der Pfad zu Gott zurück.

Hoch ist das Wort; von ihm dürft ihr nichts missen.
Was wahr ist und befreit, das müsst ihr wissen,
Und sollt es tun, und müsst es sein und lieben.
Dies ist die Lehr — in euer Herz geschrieben.

The Present

The Now in God; a thousand times I say it.
No before or after, only the ray
Of the Supreme Name that fills the heart
And stills our deepest yearning.

This is God-remembrance. Yet the day's activities
Go on; we must be brave.
Let God bear the burdens of thy daily life —
In His Name thou canst ever find repose.

The Doctrine

The edifice of doctrine is a sacred house;
You cannot dispense with its teaching words,
And think that everything resides in ecstasy;
This would be to destroy the forms of Truth.

In the beginning was the Word: bow down to earth;
Then comes the Way: half battle, half heart's delight;
Then virtue, fragrance of the soul's nobility —
Threefold is the Path that leads us back to God.

The Word is lofty: you cannot do without it.
What is true and liberating, that you must know,
Must do, must be, and love.
This is the doctrine — written deeply in your heart.

Māyā

Die Göttin Māyā hat ein Kleid genäht
Aus goldnem Stoff, jedoch mit dunklen Streifen —
Dies, weil der Schatten stets dem Hellen folgt.
Leuchten und Finsternis — wer kann's begreifen?

Ein Kleid — die Welt. Wen wollte Māyā kleiden,
Und was verhüllen? Das was ist, allein:
Verborgne Sonn die ungesehen strahlt —
Urschönheit: ja das reine, nackte Sein.

Dank

Sei nicht verfolgt von eitlen Seelenbildern;
Sei keiner Stimmung untertan.
Bewahre deine Freiheit; stehe fest
Und lass der Außenwelt den Wahn.

So wie der Adler, kreise in den Höhen —
Hat es dir nie dein Geist gesagt?
Du trägst in deiner Seel ein heilig Land —
Geh hin, wenn dich dein Träumen plagt.

Unter den Wolken mag es dunkel sein;
Darüber blüht der Sonnenschein.
In einem Wort: was macht die Seele krank?
Es fehlt ihr etwas: Herzens Dank!

Māyā

The goddess *Māyā* sewed a garment
Of golden cloth, yet with dark stripes —
For shadow ever follows light;
Shining and darkness — who can understand?

A garment — the world. Whom did *Māyā* desire to clothe,
And what to veil? That which alone is:
The hidden sun that shines unseen —
Primordial beauty: the pure and naked Real.

Gratitude

Be thou not haunted by the soul's fantasies;
Be not subdued by idle moods,
But keep thy liberty; unshakable,
And leave folly to the outer world.

As does the eagle, circle in the heights —
Has thine intelligence not told thee that?
Thou bearest in thy soul a holy land —
Go there, when idle dreams torment thy mind.

Under the clouds it may be dark;
Above them is the blossom of the sun.
Tell me: what is the sickness of the soul?
Something is lacking: heart's deep gratitude!

Satyam

Brahma Satyam, jagan mithyā:
Wirklich ist die Gottheit nur;
Schein ist, was die Welt wir nennen —
Dieses ist der Weisen Schwur.

Doch was soll der Schein bedeuten?
Etwas zwischen Nichts und Sein,
Nämlich Dasein. Und die Seele
Ist, was Brahma will befrein.

Brahmas Lichtstrahl, tief ins Dunkle:
Daseinswunder, reiner Geist
Und Erkenntnis — Tat tvam asi:

Werde, Weiser, was du weißt.

Ruf

Weil Du mein Gott bist, ruf ich Dich —
    Du wirst mich nicht verlassen.
Du bist der Hort, das Allerhöchste Gut —
    Wer kann das Höchste fassen?

Und wenn die Welt in Brüche ging —
    Du bist, was mir verbliebe.
Ich weiß nicht, was die Welt ist, was ich bin —
    Ich weiß nur, dass ich liebe.

Satyam

Brahma Satyam, jagan mithyā:
Godhead alone is Real;
What we call world is dream —
This is the wise man's oath.

What does appearance mean?
Something between naught and Being,
Namely, Existence. And the soul
Is what Brahma wills to free.

Brahma's ray, deep into the darkness:
Miracle of Existence, purest Spirit
And pure Knowledge — *Tat tvam asi:*

Become, wise man, what thou knowest.

Call

Because Thou art my God, I call Thee —
    Thou wilt not abandon me.
Thou art the Refuge, yea, the Sovereign Good —
    Who can fathom the Highest?

And though the world should fall asunder —
    Thou ever wouldst remain.
I know not what the world is, what I am —
    I only know, I love.

Shánkara

Sie, die des Denkens Fluss zum Schweigen bringt,
Göttlich besänftigend der Seele Sinn —
Sie ist Benares, ist die heilge Stadt;
Sie ist es, die ich liebe — die ich bin.

Ich bin die große Stille nach dem Tosen,
Nach Weltmeers wildbewegter Melodie —
Sprich: Friede, Friede; Herz, du bist das Selbst —

Om, Shānti, Shānti; aham Brahmāsmi.

Der Strom

Der Weg von Welt zu Gott ist wie ein Strom
Den überqueren soll die Menschenseele;
Weg von dem Ufer der Unwirklichkeit —
Auf dass die Seel sich nicht umsonst zerquäle!

Was heißt es: Mensch sein? Weg zum andern Ufer —
Durch wilde Wellen, ungestüme Wogen;
Durch Freud und Prüfung, denn es muss so sein —

Und über uns der Gottheit Segensbogen.

Shankara

She, who brings the stream of thought to silence,
Divinely giving peace to our soul —
She is Benares, the sacred city;
It is She that I love — and that I am.

I am the great Stillness after the storm,
After the world-sea's wild melody —
Say: Peace, Peace; heart, thou art the Self —

Om, Shānti, Shānti; aham Brahmāsmi.

The River

The path from world to God is like a river
The human soul must cross;
Away from the shore of unreality —
So that the soul may not torment itself in vain.

What does it mean to be a man? To cross to the other shore —
Through gentle waves and stormy billows;
Through pleasure and trial, so must it be —

And above us the rainbow of God's blessing.

Das Lob

Was heißt es: Gott loben? Es heißt, dass man weiß,
Dass alles geschiehet auf Gottes Geheiß.
Denn alles, was gut ist, hat göttlichen Kern,
Und lehrt uns die Wahrheit und preiset den Herrn.

Durch jedwelcher Schönheit beglückende Zier
Spricht Allāh zum Menschen: sei still, Ich bin hier.
Er strahlet zu uns und wir streben zu Ihm —

El-hamdu li Llāhi, Allāhu karīm!

Sprache

Gott hat dem Menschen edles Wort gegeben
Auf dass er es gebrauche und bewahre
In Wahrheit und in Würde alle Jahre —
Durchleuchtend und verschönernd unser Leben.

Bleibt auf der Höhe dieser Gottesgabe!
Mit Sprachverderbnis bleibet stets in Fehde;
Ihr könnt nichts Bessres, Edleres ersinnen
Als Meister Eckharts und als Dantes Rede.

Die Sprache ist der Seele Lebensblut —
Zusammen mit dem Geist das höchste Gut!

Praise

What does it mean: to praise God? It means we know
That all things happen at God's behest.
All that is good has a divine kernel,
And teaches us Truth, and praises the Lord.

Through the gladdening charm of all beauty
Allah says to man: be still, I am here.
He shines upon us and we strive toward Him —

Al-hamdu li'Llāhi, Allāhu karīm!

Speech

God gave to man noble language
So that he might use and preserve it
In dignity and truth throughout the years —
It illuminates and beautifies our life.

Remain at the height of this, God's gift!
Always oppose corruption of the word;
You cannot imagine anything better or nobler
Than the language of Eckhart and Dante.

Language is the lifeblood of the soul —
And with the Intellect it is the highest good.

Neuzeit

Die neue Zeit, die unsre Welt ermordet,
Kommt daher, dass man stets verändern wollte
Im Abendland. Der Osten war geordnet —
Ein Geist, ein Fels, der nicht ins Leere rollte.

Zwei Wege stehen offen dem Verstand:
Der eine geht ins Tiefe, strebt nach Oben;
Der andre sucht nach weltlich neuem Land —
Die Gier ist mit des Fortschritts Wahn verwoben.

Allmöglichkeit: es muss doch alles geben —
So lasst die Parzen unser Schicksal weben.
Du kennst das Wort, den Heilsweg — glaube mir:
Es gibt ein Paradies auf Erden: Hier!

Kali-Yuga

Aus Missverständnis ist die Welt genäht:
Da ist der eine, der den Freund verrät
Ohne zu wissen; jener sinnt auf Rache;
Keiner versteht des andern Menschen Sprache —
Kein Wunder, dass die Welt zugrunde geht.

Wir sind geboren in der Spätzeit Banden;
Unsinniges verfolgt uns bis zum Grab.
Ich hab von dieser Welt nicht viel verstanden —
Warum? Weil es nichts zu verstehen gab.

O Spätzeitmensch, sei friedevollen Mutes!
Die Zeit des Kali-Yuga hat ihr Gutes;
Gewiss, die Wirrnis dauert eine Weile —
Doch leicht gemacht hat Gott den Weg zum Heile.

Modern Age

The modern age that kills our world,
Springs from the fact that in the West
Man always has sought change. The East was in good order —
A spirit, a rock that did not fall into the void.

Two paths are open to the mind:
One is the way of depth and striving upward,
The other looks for new and worldly lands —
Greed coupled with the mania of progress.

All-Possibility: there must be everything —
So let the Fates weave our destiny.
Thou knowest well the Word, the way to salvation —
Believe me: there is a Paradise on earth, and it is here!

Kali-Yuga

The world is made of misunderstandings:
All unawares, one man betrays his friend;
The latter plots revenge;
Neither understands the other's language —
No wonder the world is falling apart.

Born in the fetters of the last days,
Absurdity pursues us to the grave.
I never understood much of this world —
Why? Because there is nothing to understand.

O man of the last days, be of a tranquil mind:
The time of the *Kali-Yuga* has its good side;
Assuredly, troubles will last for a while —
But God has made easy the way to salvation.

Welttrug

Seltsam, wie die Menschenwelt
Sich für maßlos wichtig hält.
Große Leute, hier und dort —
Mit der Zeit geht alles fort.

Falsches Glück und falsche Größe —
Schaut auf eurer Kleinheit Blöße!
Alla morte, che sarà?
Ogni cosa è vanità!

Adel

Rechthaberei auf jeglichem Gebiet
Ist Tyrannei: man will etwas erzwingen,
Auch wenn es ohn Belang.
Der Edle kann
Ein kleines Recht großmütig überspringen.

Vergesset nicht: was auch des Rechts Begier —
Die Großmut war seit je des Helden Zier.

World-illusion

Strange how the world of men
Considers itself all-important.
Great people, here and there —
In time all things will disappear.

False happiness and false greatness —
See how empty your smallness is!
Alla morte, che sarà?
Ogni cosa è vanità!

Nobility

Wanting to be right in all domains
Is tyranny: one wishes to force something,
Even if it be of no importance.
The noble man can
Renounce a petty right with magnanimity.

Do not forget: whatever one's desire to be right,
Magnanimity has always been the hero's adornment.

Sich treu sein

Mensch, bleibe was du sein sollst. Irre nicht
In kalte Fernen, um das All zu messen;
Bleib in der Mitte, wo du Mensch kannst sein;
Was dir dies öffnet, sollst du nie vergessen.

Mag sein, der Glaube ist ein Märchenbuch,
Doch er ist menschlich; er ist, was wir sind.
Unmenschlich ist das Wissen Luzifers,
Der Flug des Ikaros. Du bleib ein Kind —

Jedoch steht dir, o Mensch, die Weisheit offen:
In ihr wirst du das Höchste Gut gewinnen;
Sie irret nicht im grenzenlosen All —

Die Weisheit kommt von Oben und von Innen.

Kleinheit

Lärmendes Nichts ist manche Menschenseel —
Was bläht sie sich, als wär sie gottgeboren?
Ein kurzer Erdentraum voll Eitelkeit,
Ruhloses Tun — und alles ist verloren.

Besinnet euch: seid klein, denn Gott ist groß.
Er hat euch eine Heimat zubereitet
Im Himmelreich: ein goldner Zufluchtsort —
Wohl dem, der gegen seine Seele streitet!

Being True to Oneself

O man, remain what thou shouldst be, stray not
In cold and distant space to know the universe;
Stay in the center where thou canst be man;
What this opens to thee, thou shouldst never forget.

Maybe faith is a book of fairy-tales,
But faith is human; it is what we are.
Inhuman is the knowledge of Lucifer,
The flight of Icarus. Remain a child.

Nevertheless, O man, wisdom is open for thee;
In her thou wilt attain the Sovereign Good;
Wisdom does not wander in boundless space —

She comes from Above and from Within.

Smallness

Many a human soul is a noisy void —
Why is she inflated as if born of God?
A brief earthly dream, full of vanity,
Restless activity — and all is lost.

Remember: be small, for God is great.
He has prepared for you a homeland
In the Kingdom of Heaven, a golden shelter —
Blessèd is he who fights against his soul!

Vertrauen

Es gibt nichts Schöneres als Gottvertrauen;
Es ist der Berg, der in den Himmel ragt.
Auf Gottes Güte kannst du immer bauen,
Wenn Zweifels Bitternis am Herzen nagt.

Wenn du auf Gott vertraust, mag es geschehen,
Dass eine Prüfung dir gemildert werde;
Oder, dass Gott dir eine Gnade schenkt,
Dass du mit Mut erträgst der Prüfung Wehen.

Du musst ja ohnehin aufs Höchste schauen,
Das deinem Leben seine Sendung gibt.
Sei hoffnungsfreudig wie das Morgengrauen —
Auf dass du Jenen liebest, der dich liebt.

Der Funken

Seltsam ist das Erlebnis, Ich zu sein:
Im grenzenlosen Weltraum nur ein Funken.
Doch dieses Nichts hat Gottes Geist getrunken —
Es ist ein Tropfen von der Gottheit Wein.

Vergänglich ist der Feuerfunken — nein,
Er ist mit Gottes Gnadenstrahl vermischt.
Er ist ein Nichts, doch er kann Alles sein —
Denn er ist ewig, wenn er auch erlischt.

Trust

Nothing is more beautiful than trust in God;
It is the mountain towering to Heaven.
On God's goodness thou canst always rely,
When bitterness of doubt gnaws at thy heart.

If thou but trust in God it may well be
A trial will be eased for thee;
Or that God bestow on thee a grace,
So that with courage thou may'st bear the trial's woes.

Come what may, thou must look unto the Most High,
Who gives thy life its mission.
Be full of hope like early dawn —
That thou may'st love Him who loves thee.

The Spark

Strange is the experience of being "I":
A tiny spark in endless space.
Yet this nothing has drunk of God's Spirit —
It is a drop of the wine of Divinity.

This fire-spark is ephemeral — but no,
With a ray of God's grace it is mixed.
It is a nothing, yet it can be all —
It is eternal, even though it dies.

Der Prophet

Mohammed: spricht man diesen Namen aus,
Fügt man hinzu: Auf ihm sei Allāhs Gnade
Und Friede. Senkrecht ist der Gnade Strahl;
Waagrecht des Friedens sonniges Gestade.

Auch Kampf ist im Propheten, Heilger Krieg,
Außen und Innen, und des Lichtes Sieg.

All dies beschreibt den Guten und den Weisen:
Von Oben kommt, was Gott ihm hat geschenkt;
Doch das Empfangende, das reine Herz,
Ist einer Blume gleich, vom Tau getränkt —
Kleinod im Lotos. Lasst uns offen sein —

Ein Blumenkelch in Gottes Strahlenschein.

Erinnerung

Der Herr, mein Hirt — erinnre dich an Ihn,
Auf dass auch Er, der Höchste, dein gedenke
Und dir sein Licht und seinen Beistand schenke —
Er, welcher sprach: Ich bin das, was Ich bin.

Dinge sind gestern, morgen, fern und nah —
Gott und das treue Herz sind immer da.

The Prophet

Mohammed: when one utters this name,
One adds: Allah's Blessing and Peace
Be upon him. Vertical is the ray of Blessing,
And horizontal is the sunlit shore of Peace.

Combat too is in the Prophet, Holy War,
Outward and inward, and the victory of Light.

All this describes the good man and the sage:
What God has given him comes from above;
Whereas the receiver, the pure heart,
Is like a flower bathed with dew —
Jewel in the lotus. Let us be open —

A calyx open for God's ray of light.

Remembrance

The Lord, my Shepherd — think of Him,
So that He, the Highest, may think of thee
And give thee light and succor —
He who said: I am that I am.

Things are yesterday and tomorrow, far and near —
God and the faithful heart are always here.

Stellvertretung

Sieh einerseits: du stehst allein vor Gott;
Einsam, doch unter seiner Gnade Stern.
Sieh andrerseits: ein gotterfüllter Mensch
Steht groß vor dir, durchleuchtet von dem Herrn.

Ein Himmels- oder Erdenmensch: ein Ort
Der Gottesgegenwart, ein hohes Wort.
Du willst dich reinen Sinns zur Gottheit kehren —
Du musst auch seine edlen Spuren ehren.

Wenn euch die Meister Gottes Wahrheit geben,
Sollt ihr in ihnen Gottes Sein erleben.
Sinnbild ist Urbild. So vergesset nicht:
Der Schein des Mondes ist der Sonne Licht.
Du magst dich neigen vor dem Heilgenschein —

Du neigest dich vor Gott — vor Gott allein.

Weltschmerz

Traumschleier Welt — du brichst mir fast das Herz;
In dir sind Weisheit, Torheit, Lust und Schmerz —
Oder auch Nichts. Was nützt uns eitles Fragen?
Ein jeder muss die Last des Lebens tragen —

Die Last — das Glück. Wirf allen Kummer fort —
Dem ersten Segen ist das letzte Wort;
Anfang und Ende reichen sich die Hände —

O dass dein Herz, jenseits von Zeit und Ort,
Den goldnen Urgehalt des Daseins fände!

Representative

On the one hand, you stand alone before God;
Alone, but beneath the star of His Blessing.
On the other hand: a God-filled human being
Stands great before you, illumined by the Lord.

A heavenly or earthly being: a place
Of divine Presence, a lofty Word.
You wish to turn with pure mind toward God —
Then you must honor His noble traces too.

When the Masters give God's Truth to you,
You should feel and see in them God's Being.
The symbol is the image of the Essence. So forget not:
The moon shines with the light of the sun.
You may bow down before the light of holiness —

You bow down before God — before God alone.

World-grief

Dream-veil world — thou hast almost broken my heart;
In thee are wisdom, folly, joy, and grief —
Or sometimes nothing. What good is idle wondering?
Each one must bear the burden of this life.

Burden — happiness. Cast off all grief —
The first blessing is the last word;
The beginning and the end go hand in hand.

O may thy heart, beyond all time and place,
Find the golden content of existence!

Verzeihung

Verzeihung heißt: die Schuld ist ausgelöscht —
Der Schuldge hat verstanden, was er sollte.
Verzeihung heißt nicht, dass die Schuld nie war
Und dass der Sünder durfte, was er wollte.

Und hättest du der Sünden viel begangen
Und wärest jetzt mit Gott in tiefem Frieden —
Du solltest nichts bereun; dein Stoff ist gut
Und wird es sein im Himmel wie hienieden.

Ihr sollt nicht über das Vergangne klagen;
Die Seele ist ihr eigenes Geschick.
Ich darf und muss es immer wieder sagen:
Der Welt sind Freuden, Gottes ist das Glück.

Weihe

Wer aufwärts streben will, muss Flügel haben;
Dies ist der Sinn der priesterlichen Weihe.
Sie ist der Eingang, ist die Reinigung —
Die Seel sei über allen Trug erhaben.

Dann schenkt die Weihe eine Geisteskraft,
Denn ohne Hilfe kann man nichts erzwingen.
Es ist die Gnade, die den Aufschwung schafft —

Mit Gottes Beistand kann das Werk gelingen.

Forgiveness

Forgiveness means: the guilt has been erased —
The guilty one has understood what he must.
Forgiveness does not mean that guilt was never there,
Or that the sinner was free to do as he pleased.

Even if thou hast committed many sins,
If now thou art in deep peace with God —
Thou needst nothing rue; thy substance is good,
And will be so in Heaven, as here below.

Do not complain about things past;
The soul is her own destiny.
I may and must say time and time again:
Pleasures are of the world, bliss is of God.

Consecration

Whoever will strive upward must have wings;
This is the meaning of the priestly initiation.
It is the entrance, or purification —
The soul should be above earthly deceit.

This consecration bestows spiritual strength,
For without help, nothing can be attained.
It is grace that enables upward flight —

With God's help the Work can succeed.

Intellectus

Der Mensch, so heißt es, könne Gott nicht kennen;
Nur Gott erkenne sich. Dies heißt vergessen,
Dass Gott sich auch im weisen Menschen kennt;
Der reine Geist kann alle Rätsel messen —

Von Gott bis zum Geschöpf. Doch was er kennt,
Ist tausend Male mehr, als was er nennt.

Adam

Adam gab allen Dingen ihre Namen.
Vor seinem Geist war gar kein Standpunkt da,
Die Dinge zu betrachten, zu durchschauen —
Er nannte sie, Alpha bis Omega.

Der Mensch, als Gottes Ebenbild,
Ist fähig, jedes Ding zu nennen,
Dank eines Lichts, das aus dem Urlicht quillt —
So hat er auch die Gabe, Gott zu kennen.

In Kürze

Wo leben wir? In Raum und Zeit,
In fliehender Vergänglichkeit;
Wer sind wir denn? Ein ich, ein du,
Ein wir — und Gott ist unsre Ruh.

Die Ruh ist unser tiefstes Selbst,
Weil unser Herz der Gottesschrein.
Gottesgedenken sei die Seel:
Gebet ist unser wahres Sein.

Intellectus

Man, so it is said, can never know God;
God alone knows Himself. This is to forget:
God knows Himself also within the sage;
Pure Intellect can measure all enigmas —

From God down to the creature. Yet what It knows
Is a thousand times greater than what It says.

Adam

To all things Adam gave their names:
Before his spirit, there was no vantage point
From which to contemplate the essence of these things —
From alpha to omega, he gave names to all.

Man, as an image of God,
Is capable of naming every thing
Thanks to a light that streams out of Eternal Light —
And thus he also has the gift of knowing God.

In Brief

Where do we live? In time and space,
In fleeting transience;
Who are we after all? An "I," a "thou,"
A "we" — and God is our repose.

Repose is our deepest self,
Because our heart is the shrine of God.
May the soul be God-Remembrance:
Prayer is our true being.

Gläubigkeit

Ihr Sucher, tadelt nicht die Religionen;
Gewiss, sie haben Grenzen hier und dort;
Versteht: sie müssen ihren Glauben hüten
Und deutlich machen jedes Gotteswort —

Dem Kleinsten müssen sie's verständlich machen
Und ähnlich werden, wie die Menschen sind.
Sag nicht, dass Mythos bloße Torheit sei;
Der Alltagssünder ist ein großes Kind.

Das Dogma bietet, was die Seele fordert;
Das werden die Pedanten kaum verstehen.
Doch trägt der Glaube tiefer Wahrheit Gut;
Bist du ein Weiser, wird dein Herz es sehen.

Esoterik

Ihr sollt aus Gott nicht einen Menschen machen,
Obschon auch Menschenart der Herr muss zeigen,
Um uns zu leiten, über uns zu wachen.

Doch ist dem Herrn kein Menschenwahn zu eigen;
Auch nicht dem reinen Geist, der in uns wohnt.
Trotzdem muss er sich vor dem Höchsten neigen —

Vor Gottes Sein, das über allem thront,
Was auch sein hypostatisch Antlitz sei —
Denn wer sich neigt, den hat der Herr belohnt.

Gott ist stets neu für uns — Unendlichkeit
In tausend Schleiern — doch Sich selber treu:
Das Höchste Gut, das allem Sinn verleiht.

Belief

O seekers, do not blame religions;
True, they have limitations here and there,
But understand: they must protect belief
And render clear each word of God —

They must explain things to the simplest man,
And so they must become like men.
Say not that myths are merely foolish tales;
The common sinner is a grown-up child.

Dogma offers what the soul requires,
But this the pedants barely understand.
A wealth of deep wisdom abides in faith;
If thou art truly wise, thy heart will see.

Esoterism

You should not make a human being out of God,
Despite the fact that God assumes man's nature
In order to lead us and watch over us.

But no human folly is in God,
Nor in the pure Spirit, which dwells in us.
Still, the Spirit must bow before the Highest —

Before God's Being, enthroned above all things,
Whatever be Its hypostatic Face —
For whoso bows down, the Lord has rewarded.

God is ever new to us — Infinity
In a thousand veils — yet faithful to Himself:
The Sovereign Good gives everything its meaning.

Jivan-Mukta

Es heißt, der Jivan-Mukta sei erlöst
Im Erdenleben schon. Wer kann es deuten?
Denn Jesus und Maria konnten leiden,
Trotzdem sie selig waren, nichts bereuten.

Erlöst, befreit, ist nur der innre Mensch;
Der Äußre kann dem Weltrad nicht entrinnen,
Auch nicht der Seele Pein. Jedoch das Herz
Kann schon in dieser Welt das Heil gewinnen —

Deo volente. Streb mit ganzer Lieb
Zum Höchsten; du wirst sehen, was Er schrieb.

Bodhi

Es hat geheißen
          Nirvāna sei das Nichts.
Nicht für den Weisen;
          Der Ungelehrte spricht's.

Es gibt ein Leeres
          Das nichts ist — ohne Sein;
Es gibt ein andres,
          Das wirklich ist allein.

Und Es ist leer
          Weil jenseits aller Welt;
Es ist die Fülle
          Für den, der Es enthält —

Für den Erwachten,
          Der nicht mehr wandern muss;
O heilge Stille —
          Kleinod im Lotos, Gruß!

Jivan-Mukta

It is said the *Jivan-Mukta* is delivered
Even in this life. Who can explain?
Jesus and Mary could suffer,
Though they were holy and had nothing to repent.

Only the inner man is saved, delivered;
The outer man cannot escape the world-wheel
Or torment of soul. Whereas the heart,
Already in this world, can gain salvation —

Deo volente. Strive with all thy love toward
The Most High; thou wilt see what He has written.

Bodhi

It has been said
      Nirvana is nothingness.
Not for the wise,
      But for the ignorant.

There is a void
      Which is mere nothingness;
There is another
      Which alone is real.

And It is empty,
      Because beyond the world;
Yet It is fullness
      For him who contains It —

For the Awakened,
      Who wanders no more;
O holy Silence —
      Jewel in the Lotus, hail!

Glaube

Die Welt, ein tausendfaches Maskenspiel —
   Wer kann es fassen?
Der Weise wird das, was nicht fassbar ist,
   Gott überlassen.

Sieh zu, dass dir kein Rätsel dieser Welt
   Die Ruhe raube —
Gott weiß, aus was die Welt gewoben ist —
   Dein sei der Glaube.

Ursein

Ein Weiser sagte, Gott sei erst entstanden
Als sein Geschöpf, der Mensch, dem Wort entsprang —
Ein kühner Ausdruck, um hervorzuheben:
Ursein und Gott sind nicht vom selben Rang —

Denn mit dem Ursein hast du keine Rede;
Ein Gegenüber ist dir Gott allein.
Unfassliche Allmöglichkeit zuerst —
Dann kommt, doch zeitlos, das gelobte Sein.

Versteh: das Sein im Ursein war verborgen —
Das Sein, dein Gott: Ihn liebe ohne Sorgen.
Und aus dem Sein entsprang der Geist, erzählt
Die Schrift — der Gottesgeist; mit Ihm die Welt.

Das Schöpferselbst trägt abertausend Masken,
Und eine dieser Masken ist dein Ich.
O möge sie ein Spiegel sein für Gott —
Des Höchsten Licht bestrahl sie ewiglich!

Faith

The world, a thousandfold play of masks —
        Who can fathom it?
What is unfathomable,
        The wise man leaves to God.

Take care that no enigma of this world
        Rob thee of thy peace —
God knows what the world is woven of —
        Thine be the faith.

Beyond-Being

A wise man said that God came into being
When His creature, man, arose from the Word —
A bold expression, made to emphasize:
Beyond-Being and God are not on the same plane —

For with the Divine Essence thou canst not converse;
Only with God canst thou come face to face.
First unfathomable All-Possibility —
Then, yet outside time, comes Being, highly praised.

Understand: Being was hidden in Beyond-Being —
Being, thy God, love Him freely, without concern.
Out of Being the Spirit came — thus say
The Holy Books — God's Spirit, and with It the Universe.

Creative Being wears a thousand masks,
And one of these masks is thine own self.
O, may it be a mirror for God —
May the light from the Most High shine upon it eternally!

In Einem Wort

Die Gottheit — Sie ist Einheit trotz der Stufen:
Wurzel und Krone in dem selben Baum.
Oder dies Bild: wenn Gott die Sonne ist,
Dann ist das Ursein grenzenloser Raum.

Wenn ihr die Einfachheit nicht könnt ertragen,
So sollt ihr niemals nach der Weisheit fragen.
Zuerst: man kann nicht Gottes Wesen schildern;
Doch dann: Er strahlt es aus in tausend Bildern.

Lilā

Lilā, das Spielen
Der Welt, die träumend sich entfalten will
In tausend Spiegeln —
Des Kosmos trunknes Spiel steht nimmer still.
So ist die Seele —
Wo will der Tanz der vielen Wünsche hin?
Gedanken, Triebe,
Die vor der eigenen Verspieltheit fliehn.

Doch einmal, Herz,
Wird dieses Spiel ums Allerhöchste kreisen;
Kein Hin und Her —
Ein Gopi-Liebestanz der Guten, Weisen.
Und Krishnas Flöte
Wird unsichtbar in deinem Herzen sein;
Ein Lied von Liebe
Und Licht — des Himmels gotterfüllter Wein.

In One Word

The Godhead — It is Oneness in spite of Its degrees:
Both root and crown in the same tree.
Another image: if God is the sun,
Then Beyond-Being is limitless space.

If you cannot endure simplicity,
Do not seek Wisdom.
God's Nature cannot be described;
But it radiates in a thousand images.

Lilā

Lilā, World-Play,
Which dreamlike wishes to unfold
Into a thousand mirrors —
The Cosmos' drunken Play will never halt.
Such is the soul —
The dance of its desires, where will it lead?
Thoughts and impulses
Which flee from their own playfulness.

But finally, O heart,
Around the Highest all this play will turn;
No longer here and there —
A gopi love-dance of the good and wise.
And Krishna's Flute
Will be, unseen, within thy heart;
A song of Love
And Light — the God-filled wine of Paradise.

Yabyum

In Tibets Kunst: das goldne Götterpaar —
Die Beiden in der Liebe fest umschlungen;
Der Liebesgott, die Weisheitsgöttin: und
Ein jeder von dem Andern tief durchdrungen.

So soll es sein: die Wahrheit und der Weg
Sind eins — das Eine muss im Andern leben.
Die Wahrheit kann nicht bloß im Denken sein;
Der Wille kann nicht ohne Wahrheit streben.

Die Mitte

Der Herr sei dein Genüge — denn die Mitte
Beherrscht den unbegrenzten Raum, enthält
Was deines Herzens Liebe rastlos sucht —
In einem Punkt den Wert der ganzen Welt.

Der Lebensdurst ist eitles Hin und Her —
Wohl dem, der in Betrachtung treu verharrt
Und findet, was Begierde nimmer gibt —
Das Ruhen in des Höchsten Gegenwart.

Beides tut not; such was du brauchst im Leben;
In allem kann der Geist zur Mitte streben.

Yab-Yum

In Tibet's art: the golden Divine Pair —
The two locked close in love's embrace;
The god of love and wisdom's goddess:
Each deeply permeates the other.

Thus it should be: Truth and Way
Are one — the one must live in the other.
Truth cannot be in thought alone;
And Will cannot strive without Truth.

The Center

Let the Lord be thy sufficiency — for the Center
Dominates boundless space, and it contains
What thy heart's love tirelessly seeks —
In one point lies the worth of the whole world.

Life's thirst is idle to and fro —
Blessèd the man, steadfast in contemplation,
Who finds what desire can never give —
Repose in the Presence of the Most High.

Both are necessary: seek what thou needest for life —
In everything the spirit can strive toward the Center.

Hier und Jetzt

Mitte und Jetzt: dies sind die Arzeneien,
Die jedes weise Menschenherz erfreuen —
Und deren Bilder die Natur uns zeigt:

Da ist der Bergeshöhle Sicherheit,
Das tiefe, warme, mütterliche Innen;
Dort ist des Gipfels Unabhängigkeit
Mit reiner Luft auf schneebedeckten Zinnen.

So ist die Seel, die vor der Gottheit steht:
Wurzel und Krone —
              Doch nur Ein Gebet.

Samādhi

Verzückung, Gottesrausch — die Sinne schwinden,
        Man meint zu schweben.
Bedenke: Gnad kann auch in Nüchternheit
        Das Herz erheben —

Im bloßen Gottgedenken. Tiefes Glück
        Durchdringt die Glieder;
Urseligkeit, verlornes Paradies —
        O komme wieder!

Fern sei, dass du Gefühl der Gnade suchest —
        Dies wäre Sünde.
Doch wolle Gott, dass die verbannte Seel
        Den Frieden finde —

Den tiefen Frieden, den das Wahre schenkt
        Ohn dein Begehren —
O mög das Gottgedenken himmelwärts
        Dein Wesen kehren!

Here and Now

Center and Now: these are the remedies
That give delight to all wise hearts —
And whose images Nature shows to us.

Here is the safety of the mountain cave:
Its deep, warm, and motherly inwardness;
There is the total freedom of the summit:
With the pure air of snow-clad peaks.

Such is the soul, standing before God:
Both root and crown —
                    Yet one sole prayer.

Samadhi

Ecstasy, God-drunkenness — the senses swoon,
                    One feels like one is soaring.
But remember: also in sober states Grace can
                    Lift up thy heart —

In simple God-remembrance. Deep happiness
                    Pervades the limbs;
Primordial bliss, lost Paradise —
                    O return again!

Far be it from thee to seek a sensation of grace —
                    This would be sin.
But may God grant the banished soul
                    Find peace —

The deepest peace, that is bestowed by Truth
                    Without thine own desire —
O may God-remembrance turn
                    Thy being heavenward!

Weltschau

Ist es nicht Trübsal, dass der Weisheit Sinnen
Das ganze Weltall lässt zu nichts zerrinnen?
Vergiss nicht dieses: wer die Wahrheit kennt,
Der sieht das Gut in dem, was Welt man nennt.

Vielleicht hat eine Weil die Welt geweint —
Verklungen ihre Bilder, ihre Lieder.
Doch sei getrost: wenn du aufs Ganze schaust,
Siehst du in ihr, was ist; sie lächelt wieder.

Tiefensicht

Man spricht von Leuten: was sie wollen, tun —
Doch man vergisst dabei des Menschen Wesen.
Was ist der Mensch, was ist die Tätigkeit?
Du solltest es in der Erscheinung lesen.

Erscheinungswelt: erkenne, was du musst,
Doch sei dir auch der Dinge Grund bewusst
Und wisse, was der Geistesgabe Sinn:
Zu fassen, was die Welt ist, was ich bin —
Und was das Sein, auf dem das Ganze fußt.

Raum, Zeit und Gegenstand, Erlebnis auch:
Dies sind die Urbestände der Erfahrung;
Und dann, was allem einen Sinn verleiht —
Herzens Erkenntnis, Himmels Offenbarung.

Denn ohne Geist wäre die Welt nicht da —
Wie könnt ihr glauben, Zufall sei die Erde?
Gott und die Welt: dann sandte Gott das Wort,
Auf dass die Trennung wieder Einheit werde.

World-vision

Is it not sad that Wisdom's thinking
Allows the universe to melt into naught?
Do not forget that he who knows the highest Truth
Can see the Good in what we call the world.

It may be for some time the world has wept —
Its images, its songs, have all faded away.
But be not troubled: if thou canst see the whole,
Thou seest in the world what is; it smiles again.

Deep Vision

One speaks of people: what they want and do —
Meanwhile, one forgets man's nature.
What then is man, what is activity?
Thou shouldst perceive it in appearances.

World of appearance: know what thou must,
Also be conscious of the depth of things,
And know the meaning of the Spirit's gift:
To grasp what the world is, and what I am —
What Being is, on which all things are based.

Space, time, objects, and events:
These are the basic categories of experience;
And then what gives meaning to everything —
Heart's knowledge and Heaven's Revelation.

Without the Spirit, the world would not exist —
How can ye think the world exists by chance?
God and world: then God sent us the Word,
So separation might return to unity.

Werden

Der Traube Saft, gekeltert und gegoren,
Gibt edlen Wein und Rausch. So selbstverloren
Ist eure Seel, wenn sie zur Liebe reift,
Und wenn des Lebens Sinn das Herz ergreift.

Denn was ist Gottesliebe, wenn nicht Wein,
Himmelsgesang — nicht kalter, stummer Stein.
Das Herz ist Eis, das vor der Sonn zerfließt —
Wes Herz zerschmilzt, den hat der Herr gegrüßt.

Verharre niemals in des Zweifels Macht,
Dass der Verstand dir deinen Frieden raube.
Hast du gehört, dass Glaube selig macht?
So sprich getrost: ich glaube, weil ich glaube!

Die Güte

Die Welt: ein Strom aus Träumen, der sich schwer
Und wie verzaubert fort bewegt — zum Meer
Der ungewissen Zukunft. Ewigkeit
Harrt eines jeden, jenseits aller Zeit.

Die Ewigkeit: ein Alles, oder Nichts.
Welten des Höhenflugs, des Schwergewichts;
Doch hinter allem Schicksal Gottes Wesen —

An seiner Güte wird die Welt genesen.

Becoming

The juice of the grape, pressed and fermented,
Yields noble wine and rapture. Thus does the soul
Lose itself, when it ripens unto love,
And when the meaning of life seizes the heart.

For what is love of God if not wine,
Heavenly song — not cold, dumb stone.
The heart is ice that melts before the sun —
Whose heart is melted, the Lord has greeted.

Never remain under the sway of doubt,
Lest the mind may rob thee of thy peace.
Hast thou not heard that faith brings salvation?
So say with trust: I believe, because I believe!

Goodness

The world: a river of dreams
Moving heavily, as if enchanted, toward the sea
Of the uncertain future. Eternity
Awaits each man, beyond all time.

Eternity: it is an All, or nothing.
Worlds of high flight or heavy weight;
Yet God's Being lies behind each destiny —

And by His Goodness will the world be healed.

Natur

O Zeichen der Natur, die uns belehren —
O Schöpferwille, reihend Bild an Bild!
Der Mensch muss kennen, lieben und verehren
Was aus des Allerhöchsten Weisheit quillt —

Und werden, was das tiefe Sinnbild zeigt.
So sieh den Adler: Blitz vom Himmelreich;
Den edlen Schwan auf unbewegtem Teich —
In Demut, die sich vor dem Schöpfer neigt.
Und dann des Löwen königliche Kraft:
Man frägt sich, ob er Kind der Sonne sei.
Und dann der Hirsch mit stattlichem Geweih:
Ein Bild des Heiligen, der Priesterschaft.

Sodann die Göttin in der Form des Weibes:
Sie ist der Gottesliebe Ebenbild.
Die Botschaft ihres wundersamen Leibes
Ist wie der Wein, der uns mit Rausch erfüllt —

Damit dem Weltgetöse wir entrinnen.
O Bilder der Natur, die uns beglücken —
O möge unsre Seel aufs Edle blicken,
Und sei das Äußere ein Weg nach Innen!

Nature

O signs of nature that teach us —
O Creative Will, stringing image upon image!
Man must know, love, and reverence
What springs from the Highest Wisdom —

And become what the deep symbol shows.
Consider the eagle: lightning from Heaven;
And the noble swan on the motionless pool —
Humility that bows before the Creator.
And then the royal power of the lion:
One wonders if he is child of the sun.
And then the stag with stately antlers:
An image of the sacred and of priestliness.

Then comes the goddess in the shape of woman:
She is the image of God's love.
The message of her wondrous body
Is like the wine that fills us with rapture —

So that we escape the turmoil of the world.
O images of nature that give us joy —
May our souls see what is noble,
And may the outward lead us to the inward!

Die Nacht

Gott hat für uns die tiefe Nacht erschaffen
Mit ihrer Sanftmut und mit ihrem Schweigen;
Da ist des Mondes mildes Silberlicht
Und dann der ungezählten Sterne Reigen —

O süße Tiefe dieses heilgen Raums,
Lass aller Tage Stürme stille werden
In einem Traum von Andacht und von Liebe —

Und Friede sei im Himmel und auf Erden!

Die Lieder

Wir schöpfen nicht aus unsrer eignen Kraft,
      Wir wollen lauschen,
In tiefer Andacht selbstlos festgebannt,
      Des Meeres Rauschen.

Wahrheit und Schönheit: wir erfassen euch
      Nicht bloß im Denken;
Des Himmels Licht und Liebe möge uns
      Eur Leben schenken.

So wie die nackten Gopis, Stern an Stern,
      Um Krishna kreisen,
So möge unsrer Lieder goldner Kranz
      Den Höchsten preisen.

So fließe, Herzens Strom, vom Geist gelenkt
      Und ohne Mühe,
Sodaß die Rose, die vom Wahren zeugt,
      Vor Gott erblühe!

Night

God has created the deep night for us
With its silence and with its gentleness;
There is the moon's soft silver light
And the round-dance of countless stars —

O, sweet deepness of this holy space!
Let all the daily storms be stilled
In dreams of recollection and of love —

Peace be in Heaven and on Earth!

The Songs

Not of our own power do we create,
                We wish to harken
In deepest recollection, selfless and spellbound,
                To the sea's mighty roar.

Truth and Beauty: we grasp you
                Not by thought alone;
May the light and love of Heaven
                Bestow on us your life.

Just as the naked gopis, star upon star,
                Circle round Krishna,
So may the golden wreath of our songs
                Praise the Most High.

Thus flow, stream of my heart, under the Spirit's guidance
                Effortlessly,
So that the rose, as witness to the True,
                May blossom before God!

Der Sänger

Ihr meint, ich sei der Sänger, weil ich singe —
Weil in der Schönheit ich die Gottheit sah.
Ich bin in einen Strom hineingestiegen —
Der namenlose Sang war immer da.

Das Liebeslied ist jenseits aller Zeit —
Wer kann der Dichtung Zauber voll erfassen?
O ewiger Gesang, o Himmelsstrom,
Geboren aus dem Quell der Seligkeit —

O Andacht, die der Seele Sein vergisst
Und nur noch weiß, was Licht und Liebe ist.

Der Spiegel

Ist nicht die Welt ein Spiegel, in dem Gott
In tausend Bildern seine Schönheit sieht?
Ein Schauspiel, das vergeht, sich wiederholt —
Aufleuchtet aus dem Nichts, und dann verblüht.

Zweierlei lehren uns des Daseins Früchte:
Die Gottesähnlichkeit, die Gottesferne;
Die Ferne macht des Daseins Stoff zunichte —
Die Ähnlichkeit ist zeitlos wie die Sterne.

Excelsior

Wo wohnt der Herr? Hoch oben? Oder innen?
Ihr solltet euch auf dies gar wohl besinnen:
Gott ist zutiefst im treuen Menschenherz,
Doch stets der Höchste — schauet himmelwärts!

The Singer

Ye think I am the singer, because I sing —
Because in beauty I have seen Divinity.
I have but stepped into a river —
The nameless song was ever there.

The lovesong is beyond all time —
Who can fathom the magic of poetry?
O eternal song, O heavenly stream,
Born of the fountainhead of bliss —

O devotion, that forgets the soul's existence,
And now knows only Light and Love.

The Mirror

Is not the world a mirror in which God
Sees His Beauty in a thousand images?
A spectacle that vanishes, repeats itself —
Lights up from naught, and fades away.

The fruits of existence teach us two things:
God-resemblance and God-remoteness;
Remoteness brings to nothing the fabric of existence —
Resemblance is timeless like the stars.

Excelsior

Where dwells the Lord? On high? Or inwardly?
Reflect well upon this :
God dwells most deeply in the faithful heart,
Yet He is always the Most High — therefore look heavenward!

Gruß

Bevor ich schließe, will ich Dich begrüßen,
O Heilge Jungfrau, die mir beigestanden —
Die mir so manche Blume hat geschenkt
Und mich beglückte in der Dichtung Landen.

Und mög der Leser Deine Gnade fühlen —
Sind wir nicht Kinder dieser armen Erde?
Du bist, von Gott gesandt, der Frühlingsregen,
Auf dass die Seel zur schönsten Blüte werde.

Geist

So wie der Kreis, so ist des Geistes Wehen —
Wo ist sein Ursprung, und wer harret seiner?
Woher er kommt, wohin er geht, weiß keiner;
Ein zeitlos Rad, und nirgends bleibt es stehen —

Und ist doch reglos; Kreislauf ist nur Schein.
Denn die Unendlichkeit kennt keine Wende
In ihrem Wesen, ruht in ihrem Sein —

Der Geist ist ohne Anfang, ohne Ende.

Greeting

Before I close, I wish to greet Thee,
O Holy Virgin, who hast succored me —
Who gavest me flower upon flower,
And delight in the land of poetry.

And may the reader ever feel Thy Grace —
Are we not children of this lowly earth?
Thou art the rain of spring sent down by God
So that the soul may become a beautiful flower.

Spirit

Like a circle is the Spirit's blowing —
Where is its origin? Who is awaiting it?
No one knows whence it comes nor whither it goes;
It is a timeless wheel; nowhere does it stand still.

Yet it is motionless; its rotation is but appearance.
There is no turning in the nature of Infinity;
It rests in its own Being —

The Spirit is without beginning and without end.

Stella Maris

Ein zweiter Liederkranz

A Second Garland of Songs

Bejahung

Was ist es, was die Seel nach Innen ruft?
Was ist das Wunder, dem das Herz begegnet —
Was gibt des Friedens himmlisches Geschenk,
Was ist es, was den Geist von Innen segnet?

Es ist ein Ja zu Gott — ist namenlos,
Hat weder Form noch Grenze, ist sich freun
Am Innersten, am Daseinskern;
                       Es ist
Der Seele Wunsch, in Gott sich selbst zu sein.

Der Tag

Aufgang der Sonne, Freude alles Guten,
Goldene Botschaft, die die Erde trank;
Und dann der Abend: müde ist der Tag
Und doch beglückt, dort wo die Sonne sank.

Früh naht die Wahrheit, die Erleuchtung gibt,
Und Schönheit strahlt in unser Herz hinein.
Ein goldner Götterwagen steigt empor,
Im Siegeszug; und dann soll Friede sein.

Von Freud und Friede zeugt der Regenbogen —
Ein Bild des Segens, wie der runde Tag.
O Sonnenweg, o Wunder der Natur —
Des Höchsten Hand hat deinen Kreis gezogen.

Affirmation

What is it that calls the soul inward?
What is the miracle the heart encounters —
What bestows the heavenly gift of Peace?
What is it that blesses the mind from within?

It is a yes to God — it is nameless,
And has neither form nor limit, it is to rejoice
In the most inward, in the kernel of Existence;
                                                    It is
The soul's desire to be itself in God.

The Day

Rising of the sun, joy of all that is good,
A golden message that the earth imbibes;
And then the evening; weary is the day,
Yet blissful where the sun sinks down.

Soon comes the truth that gives illumination,
And beauty shines into our heart.
A divine chariot of gold arises
In triumphant progress; and then there shall be peace.

The rainbow speaks to us of peace and joy —
Image of blessing, like the completed day.
O path of the sun, O miracle of nature —
Thine orb was fashioned by the Hand of the Most High.

Vierklang

Vier Ströme, heißt es, sind im Paradies:
Wasser und Wein, dann Milch und Honig; sieh
Wie sich das Eine segensreich verzweigt
Und eins wird — eine innre Melodie.

Reinheit und Rausch, Güte und Arzenei —
Von jedem lebt die Seel im Paradeise.
So ist es mit dem Weg zum Höchsten Gut:
Ein jeder strebt zu Gott auf seine Weise —

Die ihm vom Allerhöchsten eingegeben;
Nur was von Gott kommt führt zum Ewgen Leben.

Stella Maris

Einst war die Seel ermüdet und betrübt —
Es war auf einem Schiff im Mittelmeere.
Die Heilge Jungfrau kam in wachem Traum,
Auf dass mich nicht der bittre Gram verzehre
Und meine Freud und meine Kräfte lähme —
Mir war, als ob des Lebens Ende käme.

O Stella Maris, Wunder auf dem Meere —
Ich wollte, dass die Reise immer währe.
Mir blieb dein Himmelsduft —
                    und deine Gnade
Ist wie der Morgenstern auf meinem Pfade.

Quaternity

In Paradise, it is said, four rivers flow,
Of water, wine, honey, and milk;
See how the One branches, rich in blessing,
Then becomes one again — an inner melody.

Purity and rapture, goodness and remedy —
In Paradise, the soul lives from each.
So is it also with the path to the Sovereign Good:
Each man strives toward God in his own way —

Given to him by the Most High;
Only what comes from God leads to eternal life.

Stella Maris

My soul was once weary and sad —
On a ship, in the Mediterranean.
The Holy Virgin came to me, in waking dream,
So that I might not be consumed by bitter grief,
And that my joy and strength might not be paralyzed —
I felt as if the end of life were near.

O Stella Maris, miracle upon the sea —
I wished the journey would forever last.
Thy heavenly fragrance remained with me —
                                    and thy Grace
Is like the morning star upon my path.

Übergang

Gelobet sei der Tag, der golden blüht;
Der Sonnenwagen ist emporgestiegen.
Gelobt sei mir die Nacht mit ihrem Frieden;
Sie hat des Tages Unruh sanft verschwiegen.

Der Tag ist Offenbarung, Offenheit,
Als ob das Leben uns zum Werke riefe;
Die Nacht ist heilig, ist Geheimnistiefe —
Ein Lied von Liebe und von Ewigkeit.

Das Spiel

Es ist so seltsam, dass die Harfe mir
So manches bringt, was meinen Geist bewegt —
Das Saitenspiel, verzaubernder Gesang,
Hat manchesmal mein Herz zum Wort erregt.

Der Quell des Wahren ist das tiefe Selbst;
Jedoch die Schlüssel zu verborgnen Türen
Sind überall. Gesegnet sei das Spiel —
Die Zeichen, die das heilge Feuer schüren.

David

Die Psalmen, und mit ihnen Saitenspiel;
Der König tanzend vor der Bundeslade;
Das Wort, die Schönheit: Bild und Klang und Tanz —
Das Überströmen vor des Höchsten Gnade.

Erfüllung der Gebote, dies ist fein,
Doch nicht genug — lieb Gott mit deinem Sein,
Mit allen deinen Kräften, sagt die Schrift —
Glückselig, wen der Rausch der Liebe trifft.

Transition

Praised be the day that golden blooms;
The chariot of the sun has risen.
Praised be the night with its deep peace,
It has gently silenced the turmoil of the day.

Day is revelation, openness,
As if life summoned us to work,
And night is holy, it is mysterious depth —
A song of love and of eternity.

The Play

Strange how the harp has brought
So much that deeply moves my heart —
The play of strings, the fascinating song,
Have many times aroused my heart to speech.

The source of Truth is in the deepest Self;
But still the keys to hidden doors
Are everywhere. And blessèd be the wondrous play —
The signs, awakening the holy fire.

David

The Psalms, with music of the harp;
The King dancing before the holy Ark;
Word and Beauty: image, sound, and dance —
An overflowing before the Grace of the Most High.

To keep the Commandments is already good,
But not enough — love God with thy whole being,
With all thy strength, the Scripture says —
Blessèd the one who by Love's ecstasy is touched.

Die Gabe

Des Wahren Strahlung, heißt es, ist im Schönen,
Es will der Weisheit Tiefe offenbaren;
Und andrerseits strebt Schönheit hin zum Wahren —
Es liegt in ihr, sich nach dem Licht zu sehnen.

Die schöne Königin von Scheba reist
Zum weisen König der Hebräer hin:
Du, Weiser, gib mir, was von Gott du weißt —
Ich will dir alles geben, was ich bin.

Die Wahrheit schenkt uns Gottes Nektar ein —
Wir schulden ihr das Ganze — unser Sein.

Heimat

Nord, Ost, Süd, West; die Heimat ist das Beste —
So sagt der Volksmund. Was die Heimat ist,
Das sagt er nicht. So ist es: man vergisst
Des Herzens Tiefe bei dem frohen Feste.

So ist es mit der Sehnsucht, die uns zieht
Nach goldner Ferne, Liebesmelodien.
O möge sie uns nach dem Einen ziehen,
Vor dem der Erdenmenschen Torheit flieht!

Wohlan: der Mensch muss eine Heimat haben,
Die muss in goldner Mitte sein.
Hier kann er seiner Seele Sehnsucht laben —
Sein Herz ist nimmermehr allein.

Sei über jede eitle Furcht erhaben —
Der Herr wird stets dein Hirte sein.

The Gift

The splendor of the true, it is said, is in the beautiful,
Which wants to manifest the depth of wisdom;
Yet beauty also strives towards the true —
It lies in its nature to yearn for the light.

The fair Queen of Sheba journeyed
To the wise King of the Hebrews:
"Thou, wise man, give me what thou knowest of God —
I shall give thee all that I am."

Truth pours out God's nectar for us —
We owe it everything — our very being.

Homeland

North, South, East, West; home is best —
So says a proverb. But where is home?
It does not say. And thus, at the merry feast,
Does one forget the depth of one's own heart.

So also with the longing, drawing us
Into a golden distance, to melodies of love.
O may it draw us to the One,
Before whom every human folly flees!

Indeed man needs to have a home,
And this must in the golden center be.
Here he can quench the longing of his soul —
Never again will his heart be alone.

Remain serene above all pointless fear —
The Lord shall be thy Shepherd forever.

Stille

Siehst du die Vögel nach dem Süden ziehn?
So ist Vergänglichkeit: dahin, dahin.
Sei still, verfalle nicht dem Trug der Zeit,
Die einen Traum an einen andern reiht.

Die Sehnsucht strebt nach fernem Anderwärts;
Im goldnen Hier verharrt das weise Herz.
Lass ab vom Traumbild unerreichter Ferne —

Du trägst in dir die Sonne und die Sterne.

Erdenschwere

Kann man die Seel nicht einfach fallen lassen
Wie einen Stein, den man für Gold gehalten?
Es heißt doch, man soll seine Seele hassen;
Man kann im Himmel nicht den Trug behalten.

Du sollst nicht mit der Seele Schwäche rechten —
Streit mit dem Bösen bleibt stets unentschieden.
So lass das Böse fallen, es ist schwer;
Und rede dann mit Gott —
                          in seinem Frieden.

Stillness

Do you see the birds migrating to the south?
Such is transience: passed and gone.
Be still, do not fall prey to the deceit of time
Which strings dream upon dream.

Our longing strives for distant elsewheres;
The wise heart abides in the golden Here.
Renounce the dream-picture of unreached lands —

You carry in yourself the sun and the stars.

Earthly Heaviness

Can one not simply drop the soul
Like a stone one had fancied to be gold?
It has been said that we should hate our soul;
In Heaven no illusion can remain.

With the weakness of your soul you should not argue —
Struggle with the Evil One is ever undecided.
So drop all evil; it is heavy:
Then talk to God —
                                    within His Peace.

Jenseits

Maria sprach zu einer frommen Seele:
„Das Glück kann ich dir nicht für diese Welt
Versprechen — für die nächste nur." Dies Wort
Birgt eine Lehre: nur das Jenseits zählt —

Das heißt: die Welt muss das sein, was sie ist;
Fürs Erdenleben zahlen wir Tribut
Dem Herrn der Welten, der die Dinge wägt.

Ihr kennet Jesu Wort: „Nur Gott ist gut."

Selbstliebe

„Und liebe deinen Nächsten wie dich selbst":
Dies heißet doch, man soll sich selber lieben;
Wär nichts in unsrer Seele liebenswert,
So wäre ihre Schöpfung unterblieben.

Die Schöpfung, Gottes edles Ebenbild.
Sich lieben, heißt: treu sein dem Ebenbilde;
Im Wahren, Schönen, ist des Menschen Heil —

Im Herzen sind die seligen Gefilde.

Hereafter

Mary said to a pious soul:
"I cannot promise thee happiness in this world —
Only in the next." These words
Contain a teaching: only the Hereafter counts —

This means: the world must be what it is;
For life on earth we must pay a tribute
To the Lord of the Universe, who weighs all things.

You know the words of Jesus: "God alone is good."

Self-love

"And love thy neighbor as thyself":
This means that one should love oneself;
If nothing in the soul were worthy of love,
The soul's creation would not have occurred.

Creation is God's noble likeness.
To love oneself means to be faithful to it;
In the True and Beautiful man's salvation lies —

Within thy heart are the Elysian Fields.

Weisung

Siehst du jemanden, der an Krankheit leidet
Oder durch ein Gebrechen ist behindert —
Bete für ihn. Du magst des öftern sehn
Ein Unglück, welches keine Tröstung lindert —

Ein kurz Gebet ist stets ein milder Strahl
Von Herz zu Herz. Sprich: Gott mag ihm verzeihn
Und helfen. Wisse, dass der Herr dich hört;
Wohlwollen soll der Seele Aura sein.

Die milde Absicht schaut nicht auf Gewinn;
Sei gut, weil Liebe ist in deinem Sinn.

Zwielicht

Ich hört einmal ein edles Lautenspiel
Voll Leidenschaft und Tiefsinn, möcht ich sagen —
Ein Lied von Sehnsucht, das vom Himmel fiel —
Wer kann die Tränen in der Lust ertragen?

Was ist das eine und was ist das andre —
Was ist des süßen Zwielichts letzter Sinn?
Dass ich durch irdische Verbannung wandre —
Und dennoch schon im Paradiese bin.

Advice

If thou seest someone who suffers an illness
Or is handicapped by some infirmity —
Pray for him. Thou may'st often see
A misfortune that no solace allays.

A short prayer is always a gentle ray
From heart to heart. Say: may God forgive him
And help him. Know that the Lord hears thee;
Benevolence should be the aura of the soul.

Gentle intention does not look for gain;
Be good, for love lies within thy soul.

Twilight

One time I heard a noble play of lute,
Full of love's depth and passion, I might say —
A song of nostalgia that fell from Heaven —
Who can endure tears in the midst of bliss?

What is the one, and what is the other —
What is the final meaning of the sweet twilight?
That I am traveling through this exile on earth —
Yet I am already in Paradise.

Liebesweise

Ein Lied erklingt so tief in meiner Seele,
Als ob es mir von Lieb und Leid erzähle —
Dieweil im Abendrot die Sonne sank,
Des müden Tages letzter, goldner Trank

Am Rand der Nacht. Kein Schlummer kommt zu mir;
Nur jenes Lied — von Liebe und von dir.
Und gebe Gott, dass alles Ihn verkünde —
Dass alles in die Gottesliebe münde.

Das Antlitz

Geliebtes Antlitz, das mein Schicksal brachte
Auf meinen Weg und in mein Herz hinein;
Es ist, was Gott seit je für mich erdachte —
Es war in Ihm, es musste ewig sein.

Ein tiefes Wort, das jede Lieb erkläret.
Gesegnet, wer sich in der Liebe fand!
Gott hat uns diesen edlen Trost gewähret —
Denn unsre Herzen sind in seiner Hand.

Minnesang

Die tiefste Liebe und das höchste Streben:
Die hat der edle Minnesang verbunden.
Wer liebt, muss Ritter sein: sich selbst besiegen
Und singen in des Kampfes grausen Wunden.

Nicht leichtes Spielen ist die große Liebe,
Nicht Träumen in der Minne süß Geheg —
Sie ist ein Glaube, strenge Heldenpflicht:
Das Weib ist nicht nur Ziel; sie ist der Weg.

Melody of Love

A song resounds deep within my soul,
As if to tell me of sorrow and of love —
While in the red of evening the sun sinks down;
The last golden drink of a weary day

At brink of night. No slumber comes to me,
Only that song — of love and of thee.
God grant that everything proclaim Him —
That everything flow into the love of God.

The Face

Belovèd face that destiny has brought
To my life's path, and deep into my heart;
From the beginning, this God conceived for me —
It was in Him: eternal it must be.

Mysterious word, explaining what is love;
Blessèd the one who, in love, finds himself!
God has given us this noble consolation —
For our hearts are ever in His Hand.

Minnesang

Deepest love and highest striving:
Both did the noble Minnesang unite.
Chivalrous must be the man who loves: conquering himself
And singing in the battle's cruel wounds.

Great love is not an easy play,
Nor is it dreaming in Love's sweet confines —
It is faith, and the stern duty of a hero:
Woman is not merely the goal; she is the Way.

Liebespole

So ist des Mannes, so des Weibes Wesen;
Des Mannes Seele liebt Unendlichkeit —
Das unerschöpfliche Geheimnisvolle,
Welches das Weib verkörpert; Seligkeit.

Des Weibes Seele strebt zum Unbedingten —
Zum Absolutum, das vom Einen zeugt;
Weisheit und Kraft, dazu Gesinnungsgröße
Und Edelmut, der sich zum Weibe neigt.

Gar manches Schöne ließe sich noch sagen —
Genug, dass wir's in unsren Herzen tragen.

Lallā

Als Lallā Yogīshwarī Ātmā fand
In ihrem Innern, war die Aussenwelt
Für sie ihr einzig Kleid, ein Traumgewebe;
So ging sie nackend unterm Himmelszelt.

So wie von außen sie nach Innen drang,
So drang das Innre in des Leibes Fülle;
So ging sie nackt und tanzend durch das Land —
Im Rausche Lakshmīs und in Ātmās Stille.

The Poles of Love

Man's nature is one thing, woman's is another;
Man's soul loves Infinitude —
The inexhaustibly mysterious
That woman embodies; beatitude.

Woman's soul strives toward the Absolute —
To what bears witness to the One;
Wisdom and strength, magnanimity,
And nobility that bows before woman.

More words of beauty could be said —
Let it suffice we keep them in our hearts.

Lalla

When Lalla Yogishvari found *Ātmā*
Within herself, the outer world became
Her sole garment, a web of dreams;
Thus she went naked beneath the vault of Heaven.

And as she entered from the outward to the Inward,
So did the Inward enter her body's fullness;
And thus she went naked and dancing through the land —
In Lakshmi's ecstasy and in *Ātmā*'s stillness.

Im Kreise

Es gibt gar manchen Weg — so Rumi sprach —
Ich wählte die Musik, den Tanz: den Pfad
Des Schönen und der Liebe; tanze, Herz!
Der Körper dreht sich wie ein trunken Rad.

Ihr neigt euch zum Gebet auf fromme Weise —
Maulânas Jünger schwingen sich im Kreise.
Gebet ist Denken und Gefühl; allein
Der Derwisch betet mit dem ganzen Sein.

Amor

Amor e 'l cuor gentil sono una cosa:
Wo Liebe ist, da muss auch Adel sein.
Das adlige Gemüt wird Liebe finden;
Da wo die Wahrheit ist, da ist der Wein.

Ein tönend Erz ist, wer nicht Liebe kennt;
In Liebe ist die Selbstsucht überwunden.
Wer je der Liebe Tiefe hat erlebt,
In ihr erlöschend — der hat Gott gefunden.

In a Circle

There are many Paths — said Rumi —
I chose music and dance: the Path
Of beauty and of love; dance, O my heart!
The body turns as if it were a drunken wheel.

Ye bow down, piously, in prayer —
Maulana's disciples in a circle swirl.
Prayer is thought and feeling;
Only the dervish prays with his whole being.

Amor

Amor e 'l cuor gentil sono una cosa:
Where there is love, nobility must also be.
The noble mind will find love;
Where there is truth, there too is wine.

As sounding brass is he who knows not love;
In love is all self-seeking overcome.
Whoever has experienced love's depth
And is extinguished therein — has truly found God.

Abend

Hast du der Nachtigall Gesang gehört
    Bei Abendröte?
Wenn alles schweigt und lauscht — ein Liebeslied
    Von Krishnas Flöte.

Es schien zu fragen jener Flöte Ton
    Im tiefen Walde,
Wann Rādhā werde ihren Krishna sehn —
    Ja balde, balde.

Ein Lied

Es gibt nicht Größe, die nicht Schönheit wirkt
    In ihrem Triebe;
Es gibt nicht Schönheit, die nicht Größe birgt;
    So ist die Liebe.

Vielleicht macht Liebe dir das Herze wund
    In stillem Leide;
Doch Schönheit wohnt in deines Herzens Grund,
    In tiefer Freude.

Sei glücklich, Herz, mit edler Weisheit Wein;
    Denn Licht macht trunken.
Der Weise ist mit seinem ganzen Sein
    In Gott versunken.

Lass, meine Seele, diese Welt verwehn
    In Gottes Weiten;
In letzter Liebe will das Herz vergehn —
    In Ewigkeiten.

Evening

Hast thou heard the nightingale's song
        At sunset, with the skies aflame?
When all is silent and is listening —
        A song of love from Krishna's flute.

Deep in the wood, the flute's sound
        Seemed to ask:
When will Radha her Krishna see?
        Soon, yea, soon!

A Song

There is no greatness that begets not beauty
        In its striving;
There is no beauty without greatness;
        Such is love.

Perhaps love wounds thy heart
        In silent pain;
But beauty dwells in thy heart's depth
        In profound joy.

Be happy, heart, with noble wisdom's wine;
        For Light inebriates.
The wise man with his whole being
        Is drowned in God.

Let, O my soul, this world fade away
        In God's infinity;
The heart will melt in ultimate love —
        For all eternity.

Seelengrund

O Nachtigall in süßer Sommernacht —
O Liebeslied, das unsre Seel entzündet!
Wer weiß, wer weiß, was Sehnsucht, Sehnsucht spricht —
Wer hat der Liebe Tiefe je ergründet?

O Liebesleid, das keine Lösung findet;
O Tröstung, die der Erde Schönheit spendet!
O Weltrad, das der Herzen Schicksal wendet;
O Liebestraum, der in das Ewge mündet!

Warum muss in der Süße Trauer sein?
Sie ist in unsre Welt hineingewoben;
Dies ist des Menschenherzens Melodei —

Die Seele sehnt sich, denn sie strebt nach Oben.

Musik

Gedicht, Tanz und Gesang und Lautenspiel —
Sprache der Kunst und Sprache der Natur.
Sag nicht, dies sei des Weltlings Freude nur —
Es zeugt von Tiefe und von hohem Ziel.

Der Schönheit und der Lieb ist Selbstsucht fern,
Und auch des Hochmuts kalte Hirngedanken.
Die Weisen, die aus Schönheits Schalen tranken,
Wandeln auf hohen Pfaden, Stern an Stern.

O Liebe, die den Gegensatz versöhnt:
Das Denken, das Erleben; Saitenklang,
Und Lied, das von der heilgen Sehnsucht sang —
O Schönheit, die der Wahrheit Eifer krönt!

O süße Weise, die ein Engel geigt —
Du offenbarest, was das Wort verschweigt.

Depth of the Soul

O nightingale, in sweetest summer night —
O love song, that inflames the soul!
Who knows, who knows what longing, longing speaks —
Who ever fathomed the depths of love?

O love-pain, that finds no cure;
O solace, that the beauty of the earth bestows!
O world-wheel, that turns the destiny of hearts,
O love-dream, that flows into Eternity!

Why in sweetness must there be sorrow?
It is woven deep into our world;
This is the melody of the human heart —

The soul longs, for it strives toward the Heights.

Music

Poetry, dance and song, and play of lute —
Language of art, and language of nature.
Say not, these are the joys of worldly men alone —
They all bespeak profundity and highest goal.

All selfishness is far from beauty and from love,
As is the cold cerebration of pride.
The wise, drinking from beauty's cup,
Walk on high trails, star after star.

O love, thou reconciler of all opposites:
Thought and experience; sound of strings
And song, that of our holy longing sings —
O beauty that has crowned the zeal for Truth!

O sweetest melody an angel plays —
Thou revealest what mere words conceal.

Heimwärts

Ein Sehnsuchtslied, das in mir weiter schwingt —
Ich weiß nicht wessen;
Ich weiß nur, dass es mir das Herz bezwingt —
Kann's nicht vergessen.

Mög jenes Lied die heimatlose Seel
Mit Gnade füllen —
Wo ist die Richtung, die uns heimwärts führt?
Im Höchsten Willen.

Maria

Der Jungfrau Hoheit hat die Schrift verschwiegen;
Denn nur des Sohnes Größe wollt man loben.
Maria sprach: „Sie haben keinen Wein" —
So sprach der Heilge Geist, der Strahl von Oben.

Der Geist, so heißt es, drang in ihren Leib;
Sie wurden Eins. Und es ist wunderbar:
Maria ist die Mutter aller Welt —
Der Strahl der Gottheit, der am Anfang war.

Vacare Deo: sie ist licht und rein,
Und dann erfüllt mit Gottes Gegenwart.
In ihr ist die Vollkommenheit des Schnees
Mit sonnengleicher Seligkeit gepaart.

Die Heilge Jungfrau ist das Gottgedenken;
Deswegen sagt der Engel: „Voll der Gnad."
Der Name Gottes, der das Herz erfreut:
Dies ist der Wein, den sie uns wollte schenken;

Und nicht nur ihre Worte, die ihr kennt —
Auch ihrer Schönheit strahlend Sakrament.

Homeward

A song of longing vibrates still in me —
        I do not know from whom;
I only know it overcomes my heart —
        It cannot be forgotten.

May that song fill the homeless soul
        With Grace —
In which direction is the homeward path?
        In the Will of the Most High.

Maria

The Virgin's majesty, the Scriptures pass over in silence;
They seek only to praise the greatness of her Son.
Mary said: "They have no wine" —
Thus spoke the Holy Ghost, a ray come from Above.

The Spirit, it is said, entered her body;
They became One. And it is wonderful:
Mary is the Mother of the whole Universe —
The divine Ray, which was in the beginning.

Vacare Deo: she is luminous and pure,
And then filled with God's Presence.
In her, the perfection of snow
Unites with sunlike bliss.

The Holy Virgin is remembrance of God;
Therefore the angel says: "Hail, full of grace."
The Name of God, which fills our hearts with joy:
This is the wine she wanted to bestow;

And not her words alone, which you know —
But also her beauty's radiant sacrament.

Kana

„Sie haben keinen Wein." Wie konnte denn
Die Heilge Jungfrau solches sagen, wenn
Sie Wein und Hochzeit nicht gewogen war?
Sie sah der Dinge Tiefe, wunderbar.

Der Dinge Wesen, göttliches An-sich —
Nicht menschliche Verkleinerung der Freuden;
Das Schöne sollt ihr leben innerlich —
Die eitle Oberfläche sollt ihr meiden.

Contemplatio

Wenn Sinn und Seele Schönes hat erlebt,
Wie kann der Mensch das Innensein erleben?
Das, was dich in der Formen Welt berauscht,
Soll dich im Herzensgrund nach Oben heben.

Gottesbewusstsein, jenseits aller Form —
Im Höchsten Namen ist das Bild vergessen.
Hier ist der Friede, den die Schönheit birgt —
Unendlichkeit — du kannst sie nicht ermessen.

Zuerst bist du es, der nach Innen schaut —
Dann ist es Gott, der dir die Brücke baut.

Cana

"They have no wine." How could
The Holy Virgin say this, when she
Was not inclined to marriage or to wine?
She saw the depth of things, miraculously —

The essence of things, the divine In-Itself —
Not human belittlement of pleasures;
You should live the beautiful inwardly —
Vain superficiality you should avoid.

Contemplatio

When mind and soul experience the beautiful,
How can a man know inwardness?
Whatever, in the world of forms, enchants thee,
Should, in the heart's depth, raise thee Above.

God-consciousness, beyond all forms —
In the Supreme Name the image is forgotten.
Here is the peace that beauty holds —
Infinity — thou canst not measure it.

First it is thou who lookest inward —
Then it is God who builds a bridge for thee.

Einklang

Wasser und Einsamkeit und herbes Schweigen;
Dem gegenüber edle Erdenfülle:
Wein, Weib, Gesang. Zuerst Entsagung, Stille,
Und dann der Liebeswonne trunkner Reigen.

Wein, Weib, Gesang; es will im Innern sein,
Was weltlich war; es will im Geist erklingen.
Das Wahre schimmert durch den Erdenschein
Und segnet unser Herz; so lasst uns singen!

O Seelengrund, in deinem Reich wird eins,
Was in der Außenwelt sich trennen musste:
Des Wassers Reinheit und der Rausch des Weins —

O Seligkeit, von der die Welt nicht wusste!

Das Weib

Warum sagt Rumi, unerschaffen sei
Sie, die wir lieben: das erschaffne Weib?
Sie sei ein Strahl der Gottheit, offenbare
Das Göttliche durch ihren goldnen Leib?

Nicht Schönheit nur, nicht nur der Seele Glück
Und mütterliche Güte offenbart
Die weibliche Gestalt, des Weibes Blick;
Unendliches ist hier mit Form gepaart.

Sie ist nicht Grenze, nicht geschlossne Tür;
Denn alle Schöpfung liegt und lebt in ihr.
Und was dem Toren bloß als Lust erscheint —

Das hat manch edles Herz mit Gott vereint.

Harmony

Water, solitude, and austere silence;
Then their opposite, earth's noble plenitude:
Wine, woman, song. First renunciation, stillness,
Then the enraptured round of love's delight.

Wine, woman, song: what was once worldly
Wishes to be inward, and resound within our spirit.
The True shimmers through earthly appearance
And blesses our heart; so let us sing!

O depth of soul, in thy kingdom is united
What must be separated in the outer world:
The purity of water and the ecstasy of wine —

O bliss, of which the world knows not!

Woman

Why does Rumi say she whom we love
Is uncreated: the created woman?
Why does he say she is a divine ray,
And through her golden body she manifests the Divine?

Woman's form and gaze reveal
Not only beauty, bliss of soul,
And motherly goodness;
The Infinite is here conjoined with form.

She is not limit, not a closed door;
For all creation rests and lives in her.
And that which to the fool appears mere pleasure —

Has united many noble hearts with God.

Alchimie

Shrī Shánkara beschreibt der Göttin Schöne,
Auf dass ihr Himmelsglanz die Frauen kröne.
Es soll dich nicht verwundern bei dem Weisen:
Er scheut sich nicht, auch das Gesäß zu preisen —
Wie eine Landschaft ist das Weib gemacht,
Brüste und Schenkel, und des Haares Pracht.
Andächtig lasst uns dieses Lands gedenken —
Shrī Lakshmī wird uns lächelnd Gnade schenken.

Schöpfungsspiel

Hier ist der Löwe, dort die kleine Katze;
Hier ist der Adler, dort das Vögelein;
Löwe und Adler schuf der Herr im Ernst —
Die Tierlein mögen wie sein Lächeln sein.

Es muss doch alles geben in der Welt:
Nicht nur das Strenge und erhaben Schöne;
Auch das, was von der Kindheit Unschuld zeugt —
Auf dass der Herr uns mit der Furcht versöhne.

Die Vögel

Der Adler ist der König in den Lüften;
Und auf dem Teich ein Priester ist der Schwan.
Das Honigvöglein lebt in Blumendüften;
Die Wiese ziert der Pfau, der Goldfasan.
Es ruft die Taube; und die Nachtigall
Erfüllt den Wald mit ihrem süßen Schall.

Sieh, wie das Eine sich in Viel zerteilt
Und doch als Eines in den Wesen weilt.

Alchemy

Shri Shankara describes the beauty of the Goddess,
So that her heavenly splendor may crown all women.
Be not astonished that this sage
Was not afraid to praise her buttocks too;
For woman's body is a landscape: breasts
And thighs, and splendor of her hair.
Let us think of this sacred land with reverence —
Shri Laksmhi will bless us with a smile.

Creation's Play

Here is the lion, there the little cat;
Here is the eagle, there the little bird;
Lion and eagle did the Lord create in earnest —
The little animals are like His Smile.

There must be all kinds in the world:
Not only the powerful and nobly beautiful,
But also that which speaks of childhood innocence —
So that the Lord might reconcile us with our fear.

The Birds

In the air, the eagle is a king,
And on the pond the swan is priest.
The hummingbird lives in the flowers' scent;
The peacock and the golden pheasant ornament the lawn.
The dove coos, and the nightingale
Fills the forest with its sweet song.

See how the One divides into the many,
And yet, as One, in every creature dwells.

Beschaulichkeit

Da ist die Feuergöttin Leidenschaft,
Die alles will besitzen und verzehren;
Und dann: die milde Göttin edler Lieb:
Sie will zum Höchsten Gute uns bekehren —
Dadurch, dass Gottesschau in Liebe wirkt.
Es heißt ja: Gott ist schön, Er liebt das Schöne.

O dass des Menschen zwiegespaltne Seel
Das Feuer mit der Seligkeit versöhne!

Magdalena

Maria Magdalena lebte nackt
In einer Höhle, nur um Gott zu loben.
Und Engel kamen treulich jeden Tag —
Und fassten sie, und trugen sie nach Oben.

Heilige Nacktheit: sie mag Armut sein
Und Weltverachtung; jedoch auch das Kleid
Der Himmelsschönheit, Gottes Ebenbild —
Das herrliche Gewand der Seligkeit.

Kurven

Schau auf den Horizont: die Welt ist rund,
        So wie der Ursprung aller Dinge.
Über die Erde gleiten Tag und Nacht
        In einem anfangslosen Ringe.

Das Weltrad, zeitlos — ewge Melodie,
        Und doch das Maß für alle Zeiten.
Traumschleier Welt, Gewebe unsres Seins —
        O Rausch der unfassbaren Weiten!

Contemplativity

Here is the fiery goddess Passion,
Who seeks to possess and devour all;
And there the gentle goddess of Noble Love:
She wishes to turn us toward the Sovereign Good —
Because the contemplation of God works in love.
Is it not said: "God is beautiful, and He loves beauty"?

O that man's divided soul
Might reconcile fire with bliss.

Mary Magdalene

Mary Magdalene lived naked
In a cave, solely to praise God.
And the angels came faithfully each day —
And caught her up, and carried her on high.

Sacred nudity: it may be poverty
And contempt of the world, but it may also be
The garb of Heaven's Beauty, of God's image —
The glorious raiment of Beatitude.

Curves

Look at the horizon: the world is round,
        And so too is the origin of everything.
Over the earth glide day and night,
        In a circle without beginning.

The timeless world-wheel — eternal melody,
        And yet the measure of all time.
Dream-veil world, fabric of our existence —
        O ecstasy of unfathomable space!

Die Sonne

Es heißt, man soll die Sonne nicht verehren,
Weil Gott allein das Große Eine ist.
Das hat wohl Sinn. Nur stellet sich die Frage,
Mit welchem Maßstab man die Dinge misst.

In einer Welt, die gegen Heiden tobte,
War San Francesco, der die Sonne lobte.

Vergöttert nicht den großen Feuerball;
Verehrt die Absicht Gottes, die ihn machte
Als Widerschein vom Einen und vom All;
Es geht nicht an, dass man das Bild verachte.

Die Sonn verschleiert Gottes Angesicht
In Raum und Zeit; sie strahlt von seinem Licht.
O Sonnenkraft, du magst die Erd verzehren —
Ursonne, mögest Du die Seel verklären!

Gold, du bist Sonne. Unter den Metallen
Ist reines Gold das edelste von allen.
„Wer Gold besitzt, es jedoch nicht verkauft,
Erreicht die Weisheit" — eine alte Lehre
Des schwarzen Volkes der Aschanti; sieh,
Dass Reichtum niemals deinen Sinn verkehre.

Das Gold ist heilig. Segen oder Fluch,
Je nach dem Menschen — er mag weise sein
Oder ein Tor. Den Sinn des Goldes such:
Es ist geboren aus der Sonne Schein.

Die Sonne und der Mond — man könnte meinen,
Ein jedes hätte sein besondres Scheinen.
Der Mond ist klein, die Sonne ist gewaltig;
Des Lichtes Spiel im Raum ist vielgestaltig —

Doch ob wir auch des Weltalls Rand erreichen:
Es gibt nur Licht, es ist ein einzig Leuchten —
Ein Strahlen, das von Gott kommt.
                                        Er allein
Vermag in Welt und Mensch das Licht zu sein.

The Sun

The sun should not be worshiped, so they say,
Since God alone is the Great One.
This has a meaning. But then there is the question:
With what measure does one measure things?

In times that against heathens raged,
There lived Saint Francis, who praised the sun.

Do not make a god of the great fireball;
Revere the Lord's intention which created it
As a reflection of the One, and of the All;
It is not right that we should scorn the image.

The sun has veiled the Face of God
In space and time; yet it shines with His light.
O power of the sun, thou may'st consume the earth —
O primordial Sun, may'st Thou transmute the soul!

Gold, thou art sun. Among the metals
Pure gold is noblest of them all.
"Whoever owns gold, and does not sell it,
Will attain wisdom" — this is an old teaching
Of the people of Ashanti. Take care
That wealth never corrupt thy mind.

Gold is sacred. It is a blessing or a curse
Depending on the person — be he a wise man
Or a fool. Seek the meaning of gold:
It is born of the radiance of the sun.

Sun and moon — one might well think
Each shines in its own unique way.
The moon is small, the sun is mighty;
The play of light in space has many forms.

But even if we travel to the universe's rim
There is only light, one sole illumination —
A radiance that comes from God.
                              He alone
Can be the Light within the world and men.

Andacht

O Sonnenuntergang — du Tor der Nacht,
Die allen Zwist in Welt und Seel versöhnt;
Du bist die Andacht, die nach Gott sich sehnt —
Ja Gottes Huld, die unser Herz bewacht.

In Gottes Geist hat alles seinen Sinn:
Tag oder Nacht, in jedem ist Gewinn;
Ātmā ist in die Welt hineingewoben —
O Strahl der Morgensonne, lass dich loben!

Die Welle

Deus est Amor — und das Gut will strahlen
In seiner Fülle, weil der Überfluss
Nach Kundgebung geheimer Schätze strebt —
Weil alles Edle sich verschenken muss.

„Gott ist die Liebe": seines Wesens Pracht
Hat Gott als eine gnadenreiche Welle
Der Welt in tausend Wundern dargebracht —

L'Amor che muove il sole e l'altre stelle!

Devotion

O setting sun — thou gate of night
That reconciles all feuds in world and soul;
Thou art devotion yearning after God —
Yea, God's Mercy watching o'er our hearts.

Within God's Spirit everything has meaning:
Both day and night, in each there is a boon;
Ātmā is woven deep into the world —
O ray of morning sun, be praised!

The Wave

Deus est Amor — the Good wishes to radiate
Its fullness, because abundance
Strives to manifest its secret treasures —
Because all that is noble must give itself away.

"God is Love": He has offered to the world
The splendor of His Being as a wave
Of mercy in a thousand marvels —

L'Amor che muove il sole e l'altre stelle!

Zigeunerweise

Zigeunervolk, rastlos — ihr geht und geht,
So wie im Herbst der Wind das Laub verweht.
Ihr wohnt auf einem nimmermüden Rade —
Anfang- und endlos sind der Wandrung Pfade.

Zigeuner, Schwermut und doch froher Sinn —
So wanderst du den Himmelsrand entlang.
Wer weiß, wer weiß, was deine Geige sang —
Endlose Melodie — woher, wohin?

Stets auf der Flucht, stets auf der Wallfahrt nach
Dem Heiligen — du tanzest, betest viel.
Das Wandern ist dein Heim; und was du suchst,
Du weißt es nicht.
          Im Herzen ist das Ziel.

Die Flucht

Die Menschen scheinen auf der Flucht zu sein —
Was ängstigt sie, was macht wohl, dass sie fliehn?
Sie fliehn nicht nur vor Fremdem, das bedroht,
Sie fliehen vor sich selbst, vor ihren Mühn —
Vor ihrem bloßen Dasein. Mensch, hör zu —
Du bist am Rand des Seins, wo gehst du hin?
Halt ein!
       Gott ist die Mitte und die Ruh.

Gypsy Melody

Restless Gypsy folk — ever wandering,
Like autumn wind scattering the leaves.
You live on wheels that never tire —
Your trails have no beginning and no end.

Gypsy, melancholy yet of cheerful mind —
Wandering thus along the rim of sky.
Who knows, who knows what sings thy violin —
Melodies without end — from where, to where?

Ever fleeing, ever on pilgrimage
Toward the sacred — dancing, and praying much.
Thy home is wandering; and what thou seekest
Thou knowest not.
                    Thy destination is the heart.

Flight

Men always seem to be fleeing —
What frightens them, what makes them flee?
They flee not only from strange things that threaten,
They flee from themselves, from their woes —
From their very existence. Listen, O man,
Thou art at the rim of Being, where dost thou go?
Halt!
        God is the Center and our Repose.

Regen

Der Allerhöchste hauchte in den Regen
Für unsre Erde Lebenskraft und Segen —
Mögen des Höchsten Gnaden für den Frommen
Wie Regenschauer in die Seele kommen!

Die äußern Wunderzeichen der Natur —
Sie sind ein Bild der innern Wunder nur.
Die Seel verdorrt in törichtem Gerede —
Gott sendet Leben in des Herzens Öde.

Der Regen, der die Erd vom Himmel grüßte,
Ließ blühen die Oase in der Wüste.

Das Meer

Sinnbilder bietet diese Welt in Fülle —
Schau auf das eine, grenzenlose Meer:
Da braust von fern der wilde Sturm daher,
Und dann ist wieder weite, tiefe Stille.

So ist die Gottheit: einsam und gewaltig,
In ihrem Wirken reich und vielgestaltig
Und dennoch Eines. Seele, schaue zu —
Find in der Wahrheit Größe deine Ruh.

Rain

The Lord Most High breathed into rain
Power of life and blessing for our earth —
May the graces of the Most High
Stream like rainshowers into the souls of the pious!

The outward wonder-signs of Nature
Are but an image of the inward.
The soul dries up with foolish gossip —
But God revives the wasteland of our hearts.

The rain from Heaven that greets the earth
Makes the oasis in the desert bloom.

The Sea

This world offers abundant symbols —
Look at the one and boundless sea:
There rushes from afar the howling storm,
And then, once more, comes vast, deep stillness.

Thus also is Divinity: alone and powerful,
Rich in Its working and manifold in scope,
Yet It is One. O soul, reflect —
Find thy repose in the greatness of Truth.

Herbst

Hier ist der Herbst — er hat das Grün verfärbt,
Und es wird kühl. Hört ihr des Windes Wehen
Im lebensmüden Wald? So ist die Welt,
Wenn alle Erdendinge leis vergehen.

Ihr hört von fern das Singen einer Flöte —
Ein Sehnsuchtslied, das in die Herzen dringt.
Dies ist der Herbst — Spätsommer, der verklingt,
Im Rausch von hellem Gold und tiefer Röte.

Seid nicht betrübt, wenn Lebens Sommer scheidet —
O Friede, der die Seel mit Gold bekleidet!

Winter

Vom Himmel kommen schwebende Kristalle —
Ein jeder eine kleine Welt für sich.
Bald ist das weite Land mit Schnee bedeckt;
Alles ist weiß, das Farbenspiel verblich.

So ist es, wenn der Trug in uns verschwindet
Unter dem Schnee der Gottergebenheit —
Der Reinheit, die das Himmelreich verkündet;
O lichte Stille der Erhabenheit.

Der Sturm

Der Sturmwind, wild und schön, der Bäume fällt
Und Wogen baut, spielt grimmig mit der Welt,
Auf Erd und Meer; wer hat dich losgelassen,
Der du zerschlägst, was deine Hände fassen?

Ist auch des Himmels Urgewalt erbost —
Im Zorne Gottes ist ein tiefer Trost!

Autumn

Autumn is here — it has tinted the green,
And it grows cool. Do you hear the wind wailing
In the life-weary woods? Such is the world,
When all earthly things gently fade.

You hear from afar the singing of a flute —
A longing song that penetrates the heart.
This is autumn — late summer, dying away
In rapture of bright gold and deepest red.

Be not distressed when life's summer takes leave —
O Peace, that clothes the soul with gold!

Winter

Dancing crystals fall from the sky —
Each one a little world of its own.
And soon the land is veiled with snow;
All is white — the play of colors fades.

Thus it is, when illusion disappears
Beneath the snow of patience, trust in God —
Of purity, announcing Heaven's Reign;
O light-filled silence of Serenity.

The Storm

The stormy wind, so wild and beautiful, fells trees
And builds waves, fiercely playing with our world
On land and sea; who let thee loose,
O thou who devastates whatever thy hands grasp?

Though Heaven's primordial powers may be angered —
Within God's Wrath there lies deep consolation.

Feuer

Die Parsen beten vor dem heilgen Feuer —
Denn es ist rein, und es gibt Wärme, Licht.
Der Brand wächst an, rast vorwärts, ungeheuer —
Die Asche, die er lässt, befleckt ihn nicht.

Schau in dich selbst: mögen der Wahrheit Lehren
Wie reine Flammen Trug und Tand verzehren.
Dem Feuer gleicht das geistige Erkennen —
Und ebenso der Liebe tiefes Brennen.

Weltraum

Eisige, schwarze Nacht; Planeten, Sonnen,
Dies alles kreisend, alles ohne Ende.
Abgründe kalten Daseins, fremdes Nichts —
Und keine Mitte, wo man Tröstung fände.

Geliebte Erde, die uns Heimat ist —
O sorgende Barmherzigkeit! Ein Zeichen,
Als spräche Gott: Hier bleibe, wo du bist,
In warmer Mitte;
                    Du wirst Mich erreichen!

Fire

The Parsees pray before the sacred fire —
For it is pure, and it gives warmth and light.
The blaze increases, rushes forward, terrifying —
It is not tarnished by the ashes that it leaves.

Look within thyself: may the teachings of the Truth,
Like purest flames, devour all deceit and foolishness.
Spiritual awareness is like fire —
So is the deep burning of love.

Cosmic Space

Icy, pitch-dark night; planets and suns,
All circle in an endless round.
Chasms of cold existence, alien naught —
There is no center where solace can be found.

Belovèd earth, which is our home —
O sign of mercy and of tender care,
As if God said: remain here, where thou art,
In this center of warmth;
                              Thou wilt reach Me!

Umgebung

Willst du im Duft der Geisteswerte leben,
Musst du mit edlen Dingen dich umgeben.
Das Hässliche kann Wahrheit nicht verleihn.
Such keinen Prunk; Schönheit kann ärmlich sein;
In Tempeln und Palästen kann das Reiche
Berechtigt sein; dein Heim ist nicht das Gleiche.
Armut und Formenadel musst du ehren;
Die schlichte Kunst des Shinto kann dich's lehren.

Wie Plato sagt: das Schöne zeigt das Wahre —
Im Formgerechten wirkt das Wunderbare.

Kleidung

Der Sinn des Kleides: erstens, je nach Willen,
Die Heiligkeit des Leibes zu verhüllen.
Sodann: ein Amt, ein Wesen kundzugeben —
Um unserm Leib ein Seelenbild zu weben;
Das priesterliche, königliche Kleid
Zeigt eine Würde jenseits aller Zeit.

Das hohe Prunkgewand mag herrlich sein —
Die Gottesgleichheit zeigt der Leib allein.

Surroundings

If thou wouldst live in the perfume of spiritual values,
Thou must surround thyself with noble things.
The ugly cannot convey the Truth.
Do not seek for opulance; beauty can be poor;
Richness is justified in palaces and temples;
Thy home is not the same.
Thou must honor poverty and nobility of forms;
The sober art of Shinto can teach thee.

As Plato said: Beauty is the splendor of the True —
The Wonderful works through rightness of form.

Dress

The first meaning of dress is the intention
To veil the body's sacred form.
And then: to manifest a nature or a function —
To weave for our body an image of the soul;
The priestly and the royal garment
Manifest a dignity beyond all time.

Ceremonial dress may be magnificent —
The body alone reveals the likeness of God.

Heiligtümer

Gebet aus Stein: dies ist das hohe Münster,
Das Innre lang und feierlich und finster —
Ein Fenster, wo das Licht sich bunt zerteilt;
Und Andacht, die vor goldnen Bildern weilt.

Des Islams Bethaus, bilderlos und schlicht —
Nach Mekka strebt der Frömmigkeit Gesicht;
Man steht und betet, Mann an Mann gereiht,
Im Duft des Glaubens, der Ergebenheit.

O Heiligtum jungfräulicher Natur:
Kein Stein, kein Teppich; Wald und Wiese nur,
Und Bergeshöhe, Sonne, tiefe Nacht —
Allüberall die Allerhöchste Macht.

Ein Heiligtum, das Gott uns hat gegeben:
Es ist nicht Fernes, es ist nahes Leben;
Wo sind die Höhen, wo die Götter thronen?
Im Leib des Menschen will die Gottheit wohnen.

Arbeit

Das Handwerk ehret; machet schön und gut
Was ihr zum Leben braucht. Nicht bloß für Geld,
Für euer Heil. Das Werk ist gottgewollt;
Es ist ein Wirken für die Andre Welt.

Und Sinnbild ist das Werkzeug und die Kunst;
Es hat ein himmlisch Urbild. Gebet acht,
Auch wenn ihr pflüget und den Samen streut —
Was ihr geschaffen, das hat Gott gemacht.

Sanctuaries

Prayer in stone: such is the tall cathedral,
Long, solemn, and dark within —
A window, breaking the light into sheaves of color;
Devotion, motionless before golden images.

Islam's house of prayer, imageless and plain —
Piety's face is turned toward Mecca;
Side by side, in rows, men stand and pray,
In the perfume of faith and submission to God.

O sanctuary of virgin nature:
No stone, no carpet, only forest and field,
Mountain peaks, sun, and deep night —
And all throughout, the power of the All-Highest.

A sanctuary that God has given us:
It is not far, it is closest life;
Where are the heights where the gods are enthroned?
In man's body the Godhead wants to live.

Work

Honor craftsmanship; make well and beautifully
All things you need for life. Not for money alone,
But for salvation. The work is willed by God;
It is a working for the Other World.

Our tools and our arts are symbols;
They have heavenly archetypes. Be mindful also
Even when ye plow and sow —
Whatever ye have accomplished has been done by God.

Menschenwerk

An Münstern ist stets etwas schief gemacht —
Absichtlich, denn man wollte Weises lehren:
Vollkommen ist das Höchste Gut allein;
Ihr sollt nicht eure Kunst wie Gott verehren.

Und dieses gilt für alles Menschenwerk:
Es tut nichts, wenn nicht alles lobenswert;
Wenn nur das Ganze von der Wahrheit zeugt —
Das Ganze ist es, was dem Herrn gehört.

Wohnorte

Es wundert mich, dass manche Menschen träumen
Von schimmernden Palästen, reichen Räumen,
Alles verziert mit Gold und Edelsteinen —
Wo ist das Glück? Man möchte eher weinen.

Zu viele wohnen in verbauten Städten,
In Häusern, die wie Babelstürme sind,
Harte und kalte Riesen — wie in Ketten
Lebt man dahin; die graue Zeit zerrinnt.

Gar manche sehen nicht, dass Gottgemachtes
Weit besser ist als Künstliches, Erdachtes —
Verstandeswelten, die der Mensch sich malt;
Der Segen liegt in Wiese, Feld und Wald —

Inmitten Gottes blühender Natur,
Oder wenn reiner Schnee bedeckt die Flur.
Der Höchste hat uns unser Heim gegeben —
Der Mensch braucht wenig, um in Gott zu leben.

Human Work

There are always irregularities in cathedrals —
This is on purpose, for thereby wise things are taught:
Perfection belongs to the Sovereign Good alone;
You should not revere art as you do God.

This holds true for all human work:
It does not matter if not everything merits praise;
As long as the whole bears witness to the Truth —
It is the whole that belongs to God.

The Home

I am astonished that some people
Dream of glittering palaces, rich rooms,
All adorned with gold and precious stones —
Where is the happiness? One would rather weep.

Too many live in cities badly built,
In buildings like the towers of Babel,
Cold, hard giants — one lives one's life
As if in chains; gray time melts all away.

And many do not see that what is made by God
Is far better than what is artificial and contrived —
The mental worlds that man has painted for himself;
Blessing lies in meadows, fields, and woods —

In God's blossoming nature,
Or when pure snow covers the land.
The Most High gave to us our home —
Man needs but little to live in God.

Beides

Des Lebens Heimat sind verschiedne Sterne,
Die Gottesnähe und die Gottesferne;
Weil einerseits sich Gott in allem zeigt —
Weil andrerseits die Welt zum Nichts sich neigt.

Bejahung schaut, was strahlt auf Gottes Erde;
Verneinung wollt, dass alles Wüste werde.

Nun, beide Sichten weisen hin zum Wahren:
Die Ferne, dass wir uns ums Heilge scharen;
Die Näh, dass wir des Schöpfers Schönheit sehen.

Der Mensch soll fest auf beiden Füßen stehen.

Wakan-Tanka

Indianertum: Natur und wilde Größe;
Kein Trug bedecket eure stolze Blöße.
Härte und Schönheit; Adler, Sonnenrad;
Kampf und Gebet sind eures Lebens Pfad.

Der Große Geist: im Himmel, in den Dingen,
In Tier und Mensch und in der Wesen Ringen;
Spiel, Heldentum, und keinerlei Gewinn —

Das Urgeheimnis ist des Ganzen Sinn.

Der Jäger

Krieger und Priester ist der Mensch zugleich —
Ein Mittler zwischen Welt und Himmelreich.
Der Mensch, wenn er vor seinem Opfer steht,
Bringt Tod; doch auch versöhnendes Gebet.

Both

Diverse stars are the homeland of our life:
The nearness of God, and remoteness of God;
On the one hand, God reveals Himself in all things —
And on the other, the world tends toward the naught.

Affirmation sees what radiates on God's earth;
Negation wills that all things turn to dust.

Both visions point toward the True:
Remoteness, so we can concentrate on holiness;
Nearness, so we may see the beauty of the Creator.

On both feet, man should firmly stand.

Wakan Tanka

Indian world: nature and wild grandeur;
No lies that cover your proud nakedness.
Hardness and beauty; eagle and sun;
Battle and prayer is your life's path.

The Great Spirit: in Heaven and in things,
In animal and man, in creatures' struggling;
Play, heroism, and never thought of gain —

The Primordial Mystery is the meaning of all things.

The Hunter

Man is both warrior and priest —
A mediator between earth and Heaven.
When man stands before his victim,
He brings death, but also reconciling prayer.

Morgenrot

Der Morgen schauert über den Zypressen,
Ein letztes Traumbild wird vom Wind verweht.
Die Lerche steigt und singt ein Liebeslied,
Dieweil der frühe Stern am Himmel steht.

Versteh, o Seel, was zarte Schönheit spricht:
Die Güte Gottes ist der Schöpfung Grund.
Dessen sei eingedenk dein tiefstes Herz —
Vom Morgenrot bis zu der letzten Stund.

Ganzheit

Wahrheit, die ganze Wahrheit, nur das Wahre —
So müssen Leute schwören vor Gericht.
So ist es mit dem heilgen Gottgedenken:
Die Andacht, ganz und nur — sonst gilt es nicht.

Denn Gott ist ganz und einzig, und Er sieht
Dich an; so sei auch Eines dein Gemüt.
Lieb Gott mit allen deinen Kräften, lehrt
Die Thora — wenn du willst, dass Er dich hört!

Religio

Schau zu, was gut in Gottes Augen ist,
Ob du seist Jude, Moslem oder Christ;
Religion ist nicht, was die Andern schindet,
„Religio" ist das, was mit Gott verbindet —

Und dies allein. Die Welt braucht manche Formen —
In Gott allein sind Ewger Wahrheit Normen.
Von beiden Quellen kannst du Heil gewinnen:
Der Glaubensheld; das Gotteslicht von Innen.

Dawn

Morning shivers over the cypresses,
A last dream-image is scattered by the wind.
The lark arises, and sings its song of love,
While the early star still stands in the sky.

Understand, O soul, what gentle beauty says:
God's Goodness is the substance of creation.
Let thy deepest heart remember this —
From dawn to the final hour.

Wholeness

The truth, the whole truth, and nothing but the truth —
Thus people have to swear before the court.
Thus too it is with holy God-remembrance:
Devotion, totally and solely — otherwise it is of no avail.

For God is total and unique, and He
Sees thee; so thy soul must also be one.
The Torah teaches us: love God with all thy strength —
If thou wishest that He hear thee!

Religio

Discern what is good in God's eyes,
Whether thou be Jew, Christian or Moslem;
Religion does not mean persecuting others,
Religio is what binds us to God —

And nothing else. The world needs many forms —
In God alone are the norms of Eternal Truth.
From both sources thou canst obtain salvation:
Heroic faith and divine Light from within.

Opfer

Seltsam, dass man in allen Religionen
Früchte und Tiere opfert, heilig Brot —
Dass Abraham sein Söhnlein opfern sollte;
Dass man dem Schöpfer bietet Blut und Tod.

Im Dasein ist ein störendes Zuviel,
Da Gott allein vollkommen wirklich ist.
So gebt Ihm etwas eurer Daseinsfülle —
Bezeugt, dass ihr von seiner Wahrheit wisst.

Nur wenn ihr gebt, ist eure Seele rein
Vor Dem, der alles gibt — das Reine Sein.

Sinnbild

Ein schwarzer Wālī hat mir einst gesagt
Zu Allāh gebe es verschiedne Pfade:
Er sei die Mitte, und die Glaubensform
Sei wie die Speiche an des Geistes Rade.

Und jede Menschenseele ist ein Weg:
Gott wollte tausend Spiegel für das Wahre.
O dass der Mensch in seinem Herzensgrund
Den tiefen Sinn des Einen Seins bewahre —

Des Selbstes, dessen Strahlen zahllos leuchten —
O selig, die das „Ich bin Ich" erreichten!

Sacrifice

It is strange that in all religions
One sacrifices fruits, animals, and sacred bread —
That Abraham was asked to sacrifice his son;
That blood and death are offered to the Creator.

There is, in our existence, a disturbing "too much,"
For God alone is perfectly real.
So give Him something of your existence's abundance —
Prove that you know of His Truth.

Only if you give, is your soul pure
Before Him Who gives all — Pure Being.

Symbolism

A black holy man once said to me,
There are different paths that lead to Allah:
He is the Center, and the different faiths
Are like spokes on the Spirit's wheel.

And each human soul is a Way:
God wanted a thousand mirrors for the True.
O would that man, in his inmost heart,
Protect the deep meaning of the One —

Of the Self, whose countless rays shine forth —
Blessèd are they who reach "I am That I am"!

Distinguo

Dein Ich sei nicht in Māyā eingeschlossen;
Über den Erdendingen sollst du schweben,
Ob du auch Wein, Weib und Gesänge liebst —
In Ātmā ist dein wahres, tiefes Leben.

Gedicht, der Laute Sang und edler Tanz —
Nicht Lärm und Übermut in vollen Schenken.
Schönheit und Liebe — Ātmās Strahlenkranz;
Nur Edles kann bestehn beim Gottgedenken.

Denn Ātmā liebt man in den edlen Dingen,
Weil sie für unser Herz von Ātmā singen.

Tantra

Wenn du in Māyās Spiel das Wahre siehst:
In einem Weib, in Dingen der Natur —
Sagt Abhinavagupta — zeigt sich Gott
In dieser Form; die Form ist Ātmā nur.

Kein Götzendienst ist dies; nein, tiefes Sehen;
Buchstabenglaube kann es nicht verstehen.

Dreiklang

„Frauen und Wohlgerüche und Gebet
Macht Gott mir liebenswert" — sprach der Prophet.
Frauen: denn sie verkörpern Lieb und Güte;
Und Wohlgerüche: Segen, welcher rinnt
Von Dingen, die von Gott durchdrungen sind.

Und das Gebet: es ist des Daseins Blüte.

Distinguo

Thine ego should not be enclosed in *Māyā*;
Thou shouldst soar above the things of the earth.
Even if thou lovest wine, woman, and song —
In *Ātmā* is thy true and deepest life.

Poems, the play of lute and noble dance —
Not noise and wantonness in crowded taverns.
Beauty and love are the garland of *Ātmā*'s rays;
Only what is noble can remain in God-remembrance.

One loves *Ātmā* in noble things
Because they sing of *Ātmā* for our hearts.

Tantra

When thou seest the True in *Māyā*'s play:
In woman, or in the beauty of Nature,
Then — says Abhinavagupta — it is God Who shows Himself
In forms; the form is none other than *Ātmā*.

This is not idolatry, but deep insight;
Those who cling to the letter cannot understand.

Triple Harmony

"Women, perfumes and prayer
Has God made lovable to me" — thus spoke the Prophet.
Women: for they embody both goodness and love;
Perfumes: for they are blessings flowing
From the things imbued with God.

And prayer: it is the flower of existence.

Lob und Dank

Hamdu lil-Lāh — man lobet Gott für das,
Was man in seinem Wesen staunend liebt;
Shukru lil-Lāh — man danket Ihm für das,
Was seine Güte unsrer Armut gibt.

Allāh ist gut: ist Schönheit — ganz an Sich,
In seinem Urgrund, seinem reinen Sein;
Und Er ist gut in dem, was seine Gunst
Uns will von Tag zu Tag aufs Neu verleihn.

Danken — denn alles kommt vom Höchsten Gut;
Und Lob: Leib, Seel und Herz dem Wahren weihn.

Bitte

Das Gotteslob, der Dank; und dann das Dritte,
Das sich aus unsrer Seel ergibt: die Bitte.

Bitte nicht nur für dich — auch für den Nächsten;
Man bittet nicht bloß um das täglich Brot.
Und meine nicht, die Bitte tät nicht not —
Auch sie ist Denken an den Allerhöchsten.

Und bitte um das Letzte Gut: um Gott.

Höhenweg

Der Mensch muss sich ans Wesentliche halten
Und so sein eignes Wesen umgestalten.
Vom eitlen Zufall, der man einst gewesen,
Muss man zu Gottes Ebenbild genesen.

Die Welt ist krumm, der Höhenweg ist grade —
Tu, was das Wort befiehlt; der Rest ist Gnade.

Praise and Thanks

Al-hamdu li'Llāh — one praises God for what
In His Nature one with deep wonder loves;
Ash-shukru li'Llāh — one thanks God for what
His Goodness on our poverty bestows.

Allah is good: He is pure Beauty in Itself,
In His Essence, in His pure Being;
And He is good in all that His favor
Gives us anew, day after day.

Thanks — because all things come from the Sovereign Good;
And praise: to consecrate body, soul, and heart to the Truth.

Petition

Praise of God and thanks to God; and then another
Prayer arises from our soul: petition.

Ask not only for thyself, but for thy neighbor too;
One asks not only for our daily bread.
And do not think that thy plea is not needed —
It too is remembrance of the Highest.

And ask for the ultimate Good: for God.

Ridgepath

Man must cling to the essential
And so transform his very nature.
From the mere accident that he once was,
He must be healed in the likeness of God.

The world is crooked, the ridgepath is straight —
Do what the Word ordains; the rest is grace.

Gesellschaft

Du bist ein Mensch, musst unter Menschen leben;
Vollkommenheit ist selten, muss ich sagen.
Die Leut sind aus verschiednem Stoff gemacht —
Ertrage sie, so wie sie dich ertragen.

Und steh vor Gott; in deiner Pflicht sei tüchtig.
Wie andre Menschen sind, ist nicht so wichtig.

Nichtwissen

Es ward gelehrt: nichts ist im Intellekt
Was nicht zuvor in unsren Sinnen war;
Ein Irrtum. Denn nur aus dem reinen Geist
Werden dem Menschen letzte Dinge klar.

Ihr sagt, der Weise sei ein Zufallsmensch
Wie andre Leute, in des Alltags Bahnen
Ein Leben lang. Gewiss, der Weise lebt —
Doch was er wirklich ist, könnt ihr nicht ahnen.

Nichts ist gewiss, so sagt ein Philosoph:
Die Wahrheit kommt vom allgemeinen Zweifel.
Ein reiner Unsinn; Wahrheit kommt vom Geist,
Nicht vom Vermuten; Skepsis kommt vom Teufel.

Gewissheit war vor allem Fragen da,
Denn aus Gewissheit ist das Herz gemacht.
Gott denkt im Herzen — „Ich bin, der Ich bin."
Wohl dem, des Herz zur Wirklichkeit erwacht!

Society

Thou art a man, and among men thou must live;
Perfection is quite rare, I have to say.
Of differing substances most people are made —
So bear with them, just as they bear with thee.

Stand before God; perform thy duty well.
How other people are is not so important.

Ignorance

It has been taught: nothing is in the Intellect
That was not first in our senses;
This is an error. Because through pure Spirit alone
Are ultimate realities made clear to man.

You say the sage is a mere accident,
Like other men, and that throughout his life
He follows ordinary paths. Clearly, the sage lives —
But what he really is, you cannot know.

Nothing is sure, a philosopher said:
Truth springs from general doubt.
This is pure nonsense; Truth comes from the Spirit,
Not from conjecture; skepticism comes from the devil.

Certainty existed before questions were ever asked;
Because the heart is made of certitude.
God thinks within the heart — "I am That I am."
Blessèd is he whose heart awakens to Reality!

Reinigung

Das Wasser reinigt: viele Riten brauchen
Das Wasser für die Reinigung der Seele,
Damit sie neu ersteh; damit sie nicht
Den Zugang zu dem Höchsten Gut verfehle.

Es gibt kein bessres Ritenwasser — steht
In einer Schrift — als Geist, wenn er erkennt
Was wirklich ist. Und dann das heilge Wort,
Wenn ihr den Ewigen bei Namen nennt.

Der Ursprung

Urwasser ist die Gottheit für den Thales;
Urfeuer ist sie für den Heraklit;
Mag sein, dass man in ihrem Namen stritt —
Jeder hat recht auf seine eigne Weise.

Feuer ist Gottes Schöpfermännlichkeit;
Wasser ist seine weibliche Natur,
Der Urstoff alles Daseins. Streitet nicht —
Vom Höchsten seht ihr eine Seite nur.

Ihr fragt, woraus des Daseins Fülle quillt —
Sie kommt aus dem, was alle Form enthält:
Der Äther — tiefsten Stoffes bestes Bild —
Uräther ist der Grund der ganzen Welt.

So in dir selbst. Du bist aus Gottes Geist
Gemacht; bist endlos mehr, als was du weißt.

Purification

Water purifies; many rites
Use it to purify the soul
So that it be reborn; so that it miss not
Access to the Sovereign Good.

There is no better ritual water — so says
A Scripture — than the spirit when it knows
What is real. And then the sacred Word,
When you call the Eternal by His Name.

The Origin

Primordial Water is, for Thales, God;
Primordial Fire is God for Heraclitus;
It may be that men have argued in their name;
Each one was right, at least in his own way.

Fire: Divine Virility, creative Power;
Water: the Godhead's Femininity,
Primordial Substance of all existence. Do not dispute —
You see only one side of the Most High.

You ask whence comes the fullness of Existence?
It comes from what contains all forms:
Ether — the best image of deepest Substance —
Primordial ether is the foundation of the world.

And so it is with thee. Of God's Spirit thou art made;
Thou art infinitely more than what thou knowest.

Philosophie

Sophisten schufen das verkehrte Denken —
Die falschen Philosophen, unverfroren
Und eitel. Doch im ganzen Griechentum
Zur Weisheit wurde Plato auserkoren;
Zuvor Pythagoras, gar tief und still —
Der Wind des Geistes wehet, wo er will.

Nicht Philosophen, sondern Misosophen
Sollt man Erfinder falscher Lehren heißen —
Die ihrem Ehrgeiz, ihrem Hochmut folgen
Und sich in ihre Wahnidee verbeißen.

Plato und Aristoteles und später
Plotin: sie überstrahlen tausend Jahre
Und mehr. Was sie gewollt, und teils getan:
Dass sich die Menschheit um die Wahrheit schare.

Wahrhaftigkeit

Satyān nāsti paro dharmah:
Nichts kann über Wahrheit stehen —
Kein Gesetz, kein Recht, kein Wollen;
Ohne Wahrheit darf nichts gehen.

Dieses gilt auch für dich selber;
Wahrheit übersteigt dein Ich.
Stell dich auf die Seit des Wahren,
Und den Lügengeist zerbrich.

Ich und Erde — ist die Enge;
Geist und Gottheit — ist die Weite.
Enge darf dich nicht beherrschen;
Wähle, Mensch, die gute Seite.

Erde ist in deinem Blute;
Mehr noch Geist vom Höchsten Gute.

Philosophy

Sophists were the creators of wrong thinking —
False philosophers, insolent
And vainglorious. But in all the Greek world
It was Plato who was chosen for Wisdom.
Before him was Pythagoras, mysterious, deep —
The Spirit bloweth where it listeth.

One should call the inventors of false doctrines
Not philosophers, but misosophers —
Those who follow their ambition and pride,
And stubbornly keep to their mad ideas.

Plato and Aristotle, and later Plotinus:
They radiate a thousand years and more.
What they wished, and in part achieved,
Was that humanity should rally round the Truth.

Truthfulness

Satyān nāsti paro dharmah:
Nothing can surpass the Truth —
No law, no right, and no desire;
Without Truth, nothing should be done.

And this holds good for thee as well;
Truth far transcends thine ego.
Put thyself on the side of Truth
And break the spirit of the false.

Ego and earth — are narrowness;
Spirit and God — are expanse.
By narowness do not be ruled;
Choose, O man, the side of the good.

The earth is in thy blood;
Still more the Spirit of the Sovereign Good.

Gewissheit

O beata Solitudo,
       Hat ein Heiliger gesagt.
O beata Certitudo,
       Sag ich, wenn der Zweifler klagt.

Wahrheit und Gewissheit — beide
       Halten innig sich umschlungen;
Sicher fühlt sich deine Seele
       Wenn die Wahrheit sie durchdrungen.

Nur die Wahrheit gibt den Frieden —
       Glücklich will ein jeder werden;
Nur der Friede zeugt vom Wahren —
       So im Himmel, so auf Erden.

Wahrheit, denkt ihr, ist gar ferne
       Wie die Sterne in der Nacht;
Nicht so. Aus der Wahrheit Stoffe
       Hat dich Gott zur Welt gebracht.

Strahl

Ein Traumgeweb in tausend Traumgeweben,
Mit Lust kommt Leid; der Tod bezwingt das Leben —
Das Weltrad dreht sich ohn Beginn und Ziel,
So wie das rätselvolle Sein es will.

Und dennoch, eine Macht die kann gewinnen
Im Spiel: der Strahl von Oben und von Innen.
Dahin die Träume, die im Licht sich lösen —
Das Nichts zerrinnt —
           es strahlt das Höchste Wesen.

Certitude

O beata solitudo,
　　　　A saint once said.
O beata certitudo,
　　　　Say I, when doubters moan.

Truth and certitude — the two
　　　　Hold each other in close embrace;
Thy soul will ever feel secure
　　　　When the Truth pervades it.

Only Truth can give us Peace —
　　　　Everyone seeks to be happy;
Only Peace bespeaks the True —
　　　　In Heaven, as on earth.

Truth, ye think, is far away
　　　　As stars deep in the night;
Nay; out of Truth's fabric
　　　　God has brought thee into the world.

The Ray

A dream-web in a thousand webs of dreams,
With joy comes grief; and death overcomes life —
The world-wheel turns without beginning, without aim,
As the mystery of Being wills.

And yet there is a power that, within this play, can win:
It is the ray come from Above, and from Within.
Gone are all dreams, dissolving in the Light —
Nothingness melts away —
　　　　　　the Highest Being shines.

Sein Wille

Mā shā' Allāh: Gott tut das, was Er will.
Dies heiße, Er sei frei — so mag man wähnen —
Weil Er der Herr ist; doch der Sinn ist der:
Ihr könnt nicht jeden Dinges Ursach kennen.

Gar mancher von den braven Theologen
Hat Gottes Bild zum Menschen umgebogen.
Nicht ein Tyrann ist Gott; quod absit. Und versteht
Dass ihr des Schicksals Gründe schwerlich seht.

Die Naht

Du magst dir sagen: wär ich nichts, zufrieden
Wär ich damit. Bedenke doch, du Tor:
Das Dasein ist, was sein will. Neig dein Ohr
Dem innern Selbst, das strahlen will hienieden.

Mag sein, das Dasein ist ein rauher Stoff —
Jedoch die Māyā näht mit goldnem Faden.
Was auch das Seinsgewebe bieten mag —
Das Weltgesetz durchdringen Māyās Gnaden.

Zwar unerbittlich ist des Alls Gebäude —
Der Dinge tiefster Grund ist Ātmās Freude.

His Will

Mā shā' Allāh: God doeth what He will.
This means that He is free — so one might think —
Because He is the Lord; yet the meaning is this:
You cannot know the cause of everything.

Many worthy theologians
Shaped God's Image into a human form.
God is not a tyrant, *quod absit*. Understand
That destiny has causes you can hardly see.

Sewing

Thou mayest tell thyself: if I were naught,
I would be content therewith. Remember, fool,
Existence is what wills to be. Incline thine ear
Unto the inner Self; it wishes to shine here below.

Perhaps existence is a rough fabric —
But *Māyā* sews with golden thread.
No matter what the web of being is —
Māyā's graces permeate the world's law.

Inexorable is the structure of the Universe —
The deepest essence of all things is *Ātmā*'s Joy.

Tiruválluvar

Shrī Tiruválluvar — ein Kastenloser —
Durfte den Göttertempel nicht betreten;
So schaut er auf des Tempels Turm von fern
Und stand verzückt in stundenlangem Beten —

Und ward ein Jīvan-Mukta, hochverehrt
Von aller Nachwelt. Sieh, was dies bedeutet:
Die Heiligkeit durchbricht die äußre Form —
Sie ist, bevor die Tempelglocke läutet.

Ein Mythos

Man hat gelehrt, der höchsten Engel einer
Sei tief gestürzt — der Höchste unter allen:
„Des Lichtes Träger." Doch dies kann nicht sein;
Ein wahrer Engel Gottes kann nicht fallen.

Die Möglichkeit des Falls trug Lucifer
Von Anfang an in sich, wie fallend Weh —
So wollt und musst er sein.
                              Die Himmelswesen
Sind unbefleckt, schuldlos und rein wie Schnee.

Tiruvalluvar

Shri Tiruvalluvar — a man without a caste —
Was not allowed into the temple of the gods;
So he gazed at the temple's tower from afar,
And stood in hours of ecstatic prayer.

And he became a *Jivan-Mukta*, highly venerated
By posterity. See what this means:
That sanctity breaks through the outer form —
It exists, before the temple bell begins to ring.

A Myth

It has been taught: one of the highest angels
Was hurled down — the highest of them all,
"Bearer of Light." But this cannot be;
A true angel of God can never fall.

From the beginning, Lucifer bore in himself
The possibility of the Fall, like descending woe —
Thus did he will and thus he had to be.
                                        Celestial beings
Are spotless, innocent and pure as snow.

Eschatologie

Es wird gelehrt, es gebe Himmel, Hölle,
In Ewigkeit. Eins nur kann richtig sein:
Das Wirkliche ist göttlich, Höchstes Gut —
Ewig kann sein das Glück, doch nicht die Pein.

Warum denn wird die Wahrheit halb gelehrt?
Der Logos weiß: kein Mensch ist gern geplagt;
Die heilge Drohung wirkt, es flieht der Sünder —
Die Höll ist wahr, weil sie zum Himmel jagt.

Mag sein, der Mensch ist klug, mehr oder minder;
Nicht, dass sein Denken alles überragt —
Niemand ist seines eignen Geists Erfinder.

Ein Wort: der Erde Herrn sind große Kinder.

Heimkehr

Apokatástasis: Rückkehr der Werte,
Der guten Wesen und der guten Dinge,
Zu Gottes Schoß, wo alles ewig war
Und sein wird, dass ihr Lobgesang erklinge.

Außerhalb Gottes kann nicht ewig werden
Was Er erschuf. Er will es nicht zerstören;
Er will in seinem Sein in Ewigkeit
Der Erdenwesen selge Stimme hören.

Des Bösen Stoff wird sich zum Guten wenden —
Im Guten muss das ganze Weltall enden.

Mahāpralaya: Auflösung der Welten.
Am End der Ende kann nur Ātmā gelten.

Eschatology

It is taught that there is Heaven or hell
For all eternity. Only one can be right:
The Real is divine, it is the Sovereign Good —
Bliss can be eternal, but not so torment.

Why then is truth only partially taught?
The Logos knows that no one suffers willingly;
The holy threat works, for the sinner flees —
Hell is true because it drives the soul to Heaven.

Perhaps man is intelligent, more or less;
Not that his thinking towers over everything —
No man is the inventor of his mind.

In a word: the lords of the earth are only big children.

Home-coming

Apokatástasis: return of all values,
Of all good beings and good things
Into the Lap of God, where everything was and will be
Eternally, so that their songs of praise resound.

What God created cannot become eternal
Outside of Him. He does not wish to destroy it;
Within His Being and throughout eternity
He wants to hear the blissful voices of His earthly creatures.

The substance of evil will turn toward the Good —
Within the Good the Universe must end.

Mahāpralaya: the dissolution of the worlds.
At the End of all ends, *Ātmā* alone remains.

So ist es

Mit vielen Dingen leben, selbst ein Ding,
Und doch allein sein in erhabnem Schweigen,
Weil Gott der Eine ist — so ist der Ring
Des Menschseins; Einheit wollte Vielheit zeigen,
Hin und zurück.
              Was soll ich andres reden?
Die Wahrheit ist das ewigjunge Eden
Im Herzen. Kein verfehltes Denken trübe

Das Wechselspiel der Weisheit mit der Liebe.

Zweifel

Im bessern Jenseits bist du nie gewesen,
Wie wir kannst du Gewissheit arg vermissen —
So spotten Zweifler.
              Ich bin Erdenmensch —
Doch wo ich war, wie können sie es wissen?

Der Gegensatz

Man frägt, ob Māyā gut sei oder böse —
Des Weltalls Traumgeweb kann beides sein.
Hier Finsternis, Verirrung und Getöse —
Dort Friede, Liebe — Ātmās Sonnenschein.

Der Strahl muss sich entfernen von dem Einen,
Um dessen tausend Wunder kundzugeben
Und eine Welt ins Nichts hineinzuweben —
Denn was bejahen will, muss auch verneinen.

Ātmā: Allmöglichkeit — das Grenzenlose.
Im Geistesgrund blüht der Gewissheit Rose.

It is Thus

To live with many things, to be oneself a thing,
And nonetheless to be alone in solemn silence,
For God is One — such is the circle
Of the human condition; Unity wished to show diversity,
Flowing forth and coming back again.
                                What else can I say?
Truth is the Eden ever young
In the heart. Let no false thinking trouble

The interplay between Wisdom and Love.

Doubt

Thou hast never been in the better Hereafter;
Just like us, thou may'st be far from certitude —
So saying, the doubters mock.
                                I am a man of this earth —
But how can they know where I have been?

Opposition

One asks: is *Māyā* good or bad?
The Universe's dream-web can be both.
Here darkness, aberration, din —
There peace and love — the sunlight of *Ātmā*.

The divine ray must distance itself from the One
So as to manifest Its thousand wonders
And weave a world into the naught —
For what seeks to affirm must also deny.

Ātmā: All-Possibility — the Limitless.
Deep in the Spirit blooms the rose of certitude.

Die Schrift

Die Heilge Schrift ist unfehlbar. Gib acht —
Sie ist zum Teil aus Menschenstoff gemacht:
Das Gotteswort will Menschensprache werden —
Es ward zur Form, die man versteht auf Erden.

Wahr ist nicht immer Wortlaut, der beschreibt —
Wahr ist das, was die Seel zum Heile treibt.

Panakeia

Warum hat Gott die Sprache uns geschenkt?
      Für das Gebet.
Weil Gottes Segen dem, der Ihm vertraut,
      Ins Herze geht.

Ein Beten ist der allererste Schrei
      In diesem Leben.
So ist der letzte Hauch ein Hoffnungswort —
      Von Gott gegeben.

Was ist der Stoff, aus dem der Mensch gemacht,
      Sein tiefstes Ich?
Es ist das Wort, das uns das Heil gewährt:
      Herr, höre mich!

Scripture

Holy Scripture is infallible. But beware —
It is made, in part, of the same fabric as man:
The Word of God willed to become human language —
It became form so that it might be understood on earth.

The wording, as it stands written, is not always true —
True is what drives the soul toward salvation.

Panacea

Why has God given us the gift of speech?
            For prayer.
Because God's blessing enters the heart of him
            Who trusts in God.

The very first cry in this life
            Is a prayer.
And the last breath is a word of hope —
            Given by God.

What is the substance of which man is made,
            His deepest I?
It is the Word that grants us salvation:
            Lord, hear me!

Symbol

Was ist ein Sinnbild? Zweierlei: es kann
Willkürlich sein, ist künstlich hergestellt;
Oder: man sieht ihm die Bedeutung an —
Sein Sinn ist das, was in die Augen fällt.

Im ersten Falle ist das Sinnbild Schrift;
Im zweiten ist es nicht bloß Sinneszeichen,
Sondern es ist etwas von dem, was es
Bedeuten soll:
    Es kann das Herz erreichen.

Centrum

Weisheit ist nicht nur Kenntnis von Gedanken,
Sondern auch Sein. Selbstzucht ist keine Bürde;
Dem Weisen ist sie tiefe Lebensform —
Wer in der Wahrheit lebt, der liebt die Würde.

Die Gottheit, die das All bewegt, ist selber
Regloses Zentrum. Und der Weise
Hat daran teil: der gotterfüllte Geist
Ist Mittelpunkt im Daseinskreise.

Guru

Guru ist Brahma. Ihr sollt nicht verstehn,
Der Meister sei die Gottheit. Seht den Mond
Mit seinem Schein — er ist die Sonne nicht;
Jedoch sein Leuchten ist der Sonne Licht.

Der Avatāra soll die Gottheit sein?
Ihr solltet es begreifen: Ja und nein.

Symbol

What is a symbol? There are two kinds:
A symbol may be arbitrary, artificially conceived;
Or else: its inner meaning one may see —
Its message is what strikes the eye.

In the first case, the symbol is a writing;
In the second, it is not a mere outward sign,
But something of that which
It signifies:
>   It can reach the heart.

Centrum

Wisdom is not simply mental knowledge;
It is also being. Discipline is not a burden;
To the wise it is a deep-rooted way of life —
He who lives in the Truth, loves dignity.

The Divinity that moves the universe is Itself
Motionless Center. The sage
Partakes in it: the God-filled spirit
Is the central point in the circle of existence.

Guru

Guru is Brahma. But you should not conclude
The Master is the Godhead. Look at the moon,
How it shines — it is not the sun,
Although its brilliance comes from the sun's light.

Are *Avatāra* and the Godhead one?
You should understand: the answer is both yes and no.

Seltsam

Von Wundern wissen Heiligengeschichten
Im Mittelalter vieles zu berichten.
Sie sind nicht immer Frucht der Heiligkeit;
Die Zeugen tragen oft der Einfalt Kleid.

Gewissen Welten, Zeiten, ist es eigen,
Dass sie das Wunderbare leicht erzeugen;
Dies liegt im Wesen, nicht so sehr der Frommen,
Sondern der Glaubenswelt, von der sie kommen.

Denn jede Religion hat eine Kraft,
Die in der Blüte Wunderbares schafft —
Nicht um uns besseres zu lehren,
Doch um den Glauben zu vermehren.
Die Wunder lagen gleichsam in der Luft —

Ausstrahlend aus des Paradieses Duft.

Tugend

Die Sittlichkeit: sie kann verschieden sein;
Sie kann mit gläubigem Gefühl gen Himmel fliegen,
Von der Gesellschaft frommem Brauch bestimmt;
Sie kann auch in der Dinge Wesen liegen,
Im Sein und nicht im Fühlen — im Erkennen
Der tiefen Wurzeln, nicht im bloßen Nennen
Von Gut und Böse, wie es euch zumute.
Es nützt die Vorschrift; besser ist die Tugend,
Entsprossen aus der Menschheit goldner Jugend.

Von Gottes Schönheit kommt das an sich Gute.

Strange

During the Middle Ages, stories about saints
Speak much of miracles.
These stories are not always fruit of sanctity;
The witnesses often wear the garb of naïvety.

It is the character of certain worlds and times
That the miraculous can easily appear;
This is in the nature, not so much of the pious,
As of the world of faith from which they come.

For each religion has a force
Which in its first bloom creates miracles —
Not to teach us better things,
But rather to increase our faith.
Miracles were then, so to speak, in the air —

Radiating from the perfume of Paradise.

Virtue

Morality can be of different kinds:
With devout feelings it can soar to Heaven,
Shaped by the pious customs of society.
It can also lie in the nature of things,
In being, not feeling — in discerning
The deep roots of good and evil,
And not merely in naming them according to whim.
Prescriptions are of use; but better still is virtue
Which rises from mankind's primordial youth.

The good as such comes from the beauty of God.

Genügsamkeit

Es ist nicht Undank, doch du stellst dir Fragen:
Warum kann allzuoft der Feind gewinnen?
Wohlan, man muss dem Bösen Spielraum lassen —
So lass die Parze schwarzen Faden spinnen.

Im Dunklen ist das helle Gold verborgen —
So sei getrost; der Herr wird dich versorgen.

Mag sein, du möchtest allzuviel verstehen —
Du wünschst, dass alles offen vor dir liege,
Weißt, dass ein Schicksal seine Ursach hat;
Du kennst sie nicht.
               Gott kennt sie; dies genüge.

Anthropos

Traumschleier Mensch — wer hat dich so ersonnen,
So wie du sein musst, was du eben bist:
Ein Wesen, das das Höchste Gut vergisst
In einer Welt, die bald zu nichts zerronnen?

Du Traumgewebe Welt, wer hat in dich
Den Menschentraum gewoben, dass er sich
An dir erfreue und in dir verzehre?
Gott gebe, dass er sich zum Wahren kehre.

Der Weise ist nicht allzusehr erbost:
Die Form, in die der Mensch hineingeboren,
Ist eben dessen Möglichkeit, erkoren
Zum Heil. So streb zu Gott und sei getrost.

Sufficiency

Not to be ungrateful, but still you ask:
Why does the Enemy so often win?
Well, one must leave some scope to evil —
Let Fate spin her black threads.

Bright gold is hidden in the dark —
So be comforted; the Lord shall provide.

Perhaps you wish to understand too much —
That all be laid bare before you;
You know that every destiny must have a cause —
This is hidden from you —
                    But not from God; this should suffice.

Anthropos

Dream-veil man — who conceived thee thus,
As thou shouldst be, and even as thou art:
A being that forgets the Sovereign Good,
Within a world that soon will fade to naught?

Dream-fabric world, who wove into thee
The human dream, to take delight
And be consumed in thee?
God grant this dream will turn toward the True.

The wise man is not overly alarmed:
The form into which man is born
Is precisely the possibility chosen for his salvation.
So strive toward God, and be full of trust.

Die Aura

Jedes Geschöpf ist da, um „Gott" zu sagen;
So musst auch du der Welt Berufung tragen,
O Mensch, der du der Erde König bist —
Weh dem, der seines Daseins Kern vergisst;

Dies tut nicht Tier noch Pflanze, ja kein Stein;
Dies tut der willensfreie Mensch allein
In seinem Wahn.
                Sprich „Gott" in deinem Wandern;
Es werde eine Gnade für die Andern.
Denn eine Aura strahlt vom Höchsten Namen —

Gebet ist Segen, ist der Gottheit Samen.

Ausblick

Ihr wähnt, das Erdenleben sei Besitz;
Nein, Leib und Leben sind gemietet.
Das nächste Dasein gibt unendlich mehr
Als was das Erdendasein bietet.

Das, was zu Torheit und zu Leiden führt,
Durchschau und meide.
Das Leiden kann nur Trug, vergänglich sein —
Der Rest ist Freude.

Das Glück ist nicht im bloßen blinden Leben;
Es ist im Beten — und im edlen Geben.

The Aura

All creatures exist in order to say "God";
So must thou too accept the world's vocation,
O man, who art king of the earth —
Woe unto him who forgets the kernel of his existence;

No animal, no plant nor stone does this;
But only man, with his free will,
In his madness.
                    Say "God" throughout thy life;
It will be a grace for others too.
For an aura radiates from the Supreme Name —

Prayer is blessing; it is the seed of the Divine.

Outlook

You think you own your earthly life;
But no, body and life are borrowed.
The next life gives us infinitely more
Than what is offered here below.

Whatever leads to foolishness and pain,
See through and avoid.
All suffering passes; it can only be illusion —
The rest is joy.

Our happiness lies not in mere blind living,
It lies in prayer — and in noble giving.

Trinitas

Geist, Wahrheit, Name — die drei hohen Wunder,
In denen Gott der Welt sich wollte schenken.
Der Intellekt, die Lehr, das Sakrament —
In ihre Tiefe sollst du dich versenken,

Auf dass sich deines Wesens Sinn erfülle.
Und möge Gott des Geistes Kräfte lenken —
Da wo die Wahrheit ist, da ist der Wille.

Pneuma

Der Mensch lebt in zwei Welten; es ist schwer
Verständlich: er ist Seele, er ist Geist.
Die Eine ist des Daseins Hin und Her;
Der Andre, der uns Höchstes Gut verheißt
In Gottes Namen, ist unendlich mehr.

Die Seele lebt, jedoch der Geist erkennt —
Er ist das Feuer, das den Trug verbrennt.
Wie seltsam: was das Leben aufgerichtet,
Wird von des Geistes Strahl durchschaut, vernichtet —

Und wieder aufgebaut im tiefen Innern —
Du sollst dich an das Sein — an Gott erinnern!

Trinitas

Spirit, Truth, Name — the three high marvels
In which God wished to give Himself unto the world.
Intellect, Doctrine, Sacrament —
In their profundity thou shouldst immerse thyself,

So that the meaning of thy nature be fulfilled.
And may God guide the powers of thy mind —
Where there is Truth, there too is will.

Pneuma

Man lives in two worlds; it is hard
To understand: he is soul and he is spirit.
The first one is the to and fro of our existence;
The second, which promises us the Highest Good
Within God's Name, is infinitely more.

The soul lives, but the spirit discerns —
It is the fire that devours all illusion.
How strange: what life has first erected,
Will be discerned and destroyed by the spirit's ray —

And then deep within thee it will be built again —
Thou shouldst remember Being — thou shouldst remember God!

Upāya

Zweierlei Weisen gibt es, euch zu ziehen
Zum Weg des Heils, den Weg des Falls zu fliehen.
Zwei heilige Arzneien: lasst mich nennen
Plato und Shánkara mit herber Rede,
Die Lehren, die der Torheit Trug verbrennen —
Dann Davids, Krishnas, süße Zauberflöte:

Euch zu erleuchten, dann auch zu beschwören —
Wort und Musik; ihr sollt auf beides hören!

Zufriedenheit

Zufrieden sein mit Gott — ein schweres Wort.
Heißt es, man solle alle Welt verachten?
Wohl kaum. Gott schuf uns Menschen, uns zu lieben —
Doch innig nach dem Höchsten Gut zu trachten.

Ein golden Kleinod strahlt in unsrem Innern,
Sobald wir uns an Das, was ist, erinnern.
An Das, was ist — o Seele, sei zufrieden;
Das Paradies erblüht dir schon hienieden.

Vanitas

Zuvieles und zu wenig denkt der Mensch —
Er träumt von Wissenschaft und Weltgeschichte,
Von eitler Größe und von kleinem Kram;
Er baut Kultur und macht sie dann zunichte —

Dieweil die Erd sich um sich selber dreht,
Sich fortbewegt und um die Sonne geht.

Upaya

There are two ways to draw you to the path
Of salvation, and to flee the Fall.
Two sacred remedies: let me first name
Plato and Shankara with their stern speech;
Their teachings burn through foolish illusions —
Then the sweet and magic flute of David and Krishna:

To captivate and to enlighten you —
Words and music: you should pay heed to both!

Contentment

To be content with God — these are weighty words.
Do they mean that one should despise all things?
This is hardly so. God created us to love us —
But also for us to strive fervently toward the Sovereign Good.

Within us shines a golden jewel
As soon as we remember That which is.
With That which is, O soul, be thou content;
Paradise blooms for thee already here below.

Vanitas

Man thinks too much, and he thinks too little —
He dreams of science and world history,
Of empty greatness and of little trifles;
He creates culture and then destroys it —

Meanwhile the earth turns on itself,
Moves on, and goes around the sun.

Das Fest

Ein weltlich Fest: Lampenkristalle schimmern
　　　Im großen Saal —
Und glänzende Gesellschaft, Damen, Herrn,
　　　Sitzen beim Mahl.
Man spricht von allem und man spricht von nichts —
　　　Der Wein ist rot,
Und so der Blumenschmuck.
　　　　　　Doch keiner, keiner
　　　Denkt an den Tod.

Alltag

Der Alltag: Lärm, fliehende Menschenflut;
　　　Und Hässlichkeit
Der Räume und der Dinge; alles rennt
　　　Und alles schreit
Für nichts. Eitles Gelächter mildert
　　　Nicht diese Not.
Keiner ist edlen Sinns.
　　　　　　Doch einer, einer —
　　　Er denkt an Gott.

Die Wache

„Hört ihr Leute, lasst euch sagen:
Unsre Uhr hat zwölf geschlagen;
Zwölf ist der Apostel Zahl" —
Nächtlings bis zum Morgenstrahl,

Pflichtgetreu und Stund für Stund
Macht der Wächter seine Runde,
Singt den Leuten, was die Zeit —

Seid auch stets für Gott bereit!

The Celebration

A worldly banquet: chandeliers glitter
      In the large hall —
And brilliant society, ladies and gentlemen
      Sit down for the meal.
They talk of everything and they talk of nothing —
      The wine is red,
And so are the flowers.
              But no one, no one
      Thinks of death.

Weekday

Weekday: noise, fleeing flood of humanity,
      And ugliness
Of rooms and objects; everybody runs
      And everybody yells
For nothing. Vain laughter does not ease
      This misery.
No one is of noble mind.
              Yet someone, someone —
      Thinks of God.

The Night Watchman

"Hear ye, people, let it be known:
Our clock has now struck twelve;
Twelve is the number of the Apostles" —
Nightly, till the morning light,

And dutifully, hour by hour,
The night watchman makes his round,
Sings out the time for all to hear —

At every hour be ready for God!

Culpa

Nicht jeder Mensch ist schlecht, dies ist gewiss,
Jedoch vergiftet ist das Erdenwesen;
„Niemand ist gut, es sei denn Gott allein,"
Sprach Jesus — er, vom Höchsten auserlesen.

Nicht unbegreiflich ist der Frage Kern:
Alles Erschaffne ist dem Schöpfer fern,
Sonst wär es Gott. Wer sich vom Herrn lässt leiten,
Der weiß: die Seel muss mit sich selber streiten.

Erbsünde, sagt ihr; dies ist nicht genug.
Die Welt ist Māyā: Strahlung, doch auch Trug.

Tierheit

Die Menschheit, heißt es, ist vernunftbegabt,
Ihr Geist ist frei, steht an des Himmels Tür;
Gleichzeitig jedoch — wer kann's leugnen wollen —
Ist auch der Mensch ein unvernünftig Tier,

Das seiner Lust folgt, stolz auf eitle Dinge;
Er tut, als wären Kriege nur ein Spass
Und meint, dies könne endlos weiter gehen —

Anstatt zu „beten ohne Unterlass."

Culpa

It is certain not every man is bad,
Yet earthly being is poisoned;
"There is none good but God," so Jesus said —
He, who was chosen by the Most High.

The kernel of the question is not hard to understand:
All created things from the Creator are remote,
Otherwise they would be God. Who lets himself be guided by the Lord,
Knows: the soul must struggle with itself.

Original sin, you say; but this is not enough.
The world is *Māyā*: divine Ray, and yet illusion.

Animality

Mankind, they say, with reason is endowed,
Its spirit is free, it stands at Heaven's door;
At the same time — who can deny it? —
Man is an irrational animal,

Yielding to his desires and proud of vanities;
He acts as if wars were a simple joke
And thinks this can go on forever —

Instead of "praying without ceasing."

Spätwelt

Du wirst in eine Welt hineingeboren
Die nichts versteht, von der du nichts verstehst.
Verfälschen will sie dich nach ihrem Bilde;
Es ist ihr Wunsch, dass du zugrunde gehst.

So musst du kämpfen, um dir treu zu bleiben:
Um das zu werden, was du bist im Grunde.
Du bist halb Siegesrausch, halb tiefe Wunde;
Dies wird dich in dein wahres Wesen treiben —

O felix culpa! Denn des Bösen Triebe
Eröffneten den Weg zu Licht und Liebe.

Der Dichter

Ein Strahl kommt über dich und macht dich dichten
Am frühen Morgen und in tiefer Nacht;
Du Müder möchtest ruhn — du musst verrichten
Das Werk, das stets aufs Neu der Geist entfacht.

Wohlan, lasst mich des Geistes Stimme hören —
Gott möge meine Kleinmut mir verzeihn.
Ich will nicht gottgewollte Gabe stören —
Was Er von mir erwartet, will ich sein.

Nebenbei

Dichten ist Botschaft — oder bloße Kunst,
Ein Wörterspiel, vor dem man sich verneigt;
Ich möchte lieber sein ein Bänkelsänger,
Der einen Weg zum Höchsten Gute zeigt.

Modern World

Thou art born into a world that understands nothing,
And of which thou dost nothing understand.
It seeks to falsify thee according to its image;
It is its wish that thou shouldst be destroyed.

Therefore thou must struggle to be true to thyself:
To become what thou art within thy depth.
Thou art half victory-exaltation, half deep wound;
This will drive thee into thy true substance —

O *felix culpa*! For the cunning of the Evil One
Opened for thee the way to Light and Love.

The Poet

A ray comes over thee and makes thee write poetry
At early dawn, and deep into the night;
Thou weary one, who wouldst repose — thou must accomplish
The work, which the Spirit ever kindles anew.

Let me then harken to the Spirit's voice —
And my despondency may God forgive.
I do not wish to interfere with a God-given gift —
What He expects of me, that I will be.

By the Way

Poetry is a message — or else merely art,
A play of words, before which one bows;
I would rather be a minstrel in the streets
Who proclaims a way to the Highest Good.

Narziss - Euterpe

Jugendgedichte: allzuoft Gemisch —
Verwilderung entstellt das edle Wesen.
Narkissos ist der Dämon früher Jahre —
Gott und Erfahrung hilft uns, zu genesen.

Lyrik ist recht, doch muss sie etwas geben;
Was nicht bereichert, hat kein Recht aufs Leben.
Euterpes Wort ist aus dem Geist geboren;
Den Dichter hat der Himmel auserkoren.

Narziss, des Spiegelbild ihm Lieb entfachte;
Euterpe: Muse, die die Lyrik brachte —
Ihr wird der Flöte Zauber beigesellt;
Wort, Himmelsklang — des Krishna goldne Welt.

Dichtung

Das Zeitrad rollt und bringet mir Gedichte,
Auf dass der Geist des Menschen Torheit richte;
Auch andre, die von Licht und Liebe singen
Und meiner Seel des Himmels Tröstung bringen.

Des Daseins Härte zwingt die Poesie
So mancher Lebensrätsel zu gedenken;
Von Blumen und von Frauen möchte sie
Euch singen, einen Gruß vom Himmel schenken —

Etwas von Schönheit, Güte, reinem Glück —
Und was ihr gebt, das gibt euch Gott zurück.

Narcissus - Euterpe

Poems of youth: all too often they are mixed —
Indiscipline disfigures nobleness.
Narcissus is the demon of the young —
God and experience help us to recover.

A lyric poem is good, but it must give something;
What does not enrich, has no right to exist.
Euterpe's word is born of the Spirit;
By Heaven has the poet been chosen.

Narcissus, whose reflection stirred up love;
Euterpe: the Muse who brought the lyric poem —
With her is joined the magic of the flute,
Words, heavenly music — Shri Krishna's golden world.

Poetry

The wheel of time rolls on and brings me poems,
So that the Spirit may discern the foolishness of men;
And other poems too, that sing of Light and Love,
And bring Heaven's sweet solace to my soul.

The harshness of existence forces poetry
To consider the many puzzles of this life.
Poems wish to sing of flowers and of women,
And bring to you a greeting from Above —

Something of beauty, goodness, and pure bliss —
Whatever you may give, God gives it back to you.

Für sich

Jedes Gedicht ist eine Welt für sich.
Es gibt wohl manche, die zusammen blühen —
Doch jede Einzelbotschaft ist für dich
Und will allein durch deine Seele ziehen.

Einmalig ist der Rede Sinn geschenkt;
Ein Vorher und ein Nachher gibt es nicht —
So wie ein Lied, das deine Liebe tränkt,
Einmalig zu der Seele spricht.

Herbstlaub

Herbstblätter — was ist dieses Bildes Sinn?
Gedichte kommen spät zu meinem Ohre,
Ich weiß nicht wie — ihr Quell ist Licht und Liebe —
Tutti i miei pensier parlan d'amore.

Frühling und Herbst: Pole in Daseins Raum —
Ins Alter hat das Schicksal mich gelenkt.
Müde und selbstlos ist des Lebens Baum —
Herbstblätter sind wie Gold, das sich verschenkt.

Unto Itself

Each poem is a world unto itself.
Some of them may bloom together —
Yet each one is for thee a single message,
And wants to flow through thy soul on its own.

The meaning of each is a unique gift,
There is neither a "before" nor an "after" —
Just as a song that nourishes thy love
Speaks to thy soul in its own way.

Autumn Leaves

Autumn leaves — what is the meaning of this image?
Poems come, tardy, to my ear,
I know not how — their source is Light and Love —
Tutti i miei pensier parlan d'amore.

Spring and autumn: poles in the space of existence —
Destiny has brought me to old age.
Weary and selfless is life's tree —
Autumn leaves are like gold that gives itself away.

Lebenswerk

Das Werk: ein lebenslanger Kampf — zuerst
Ein Jugendtraum: das Wahre und das Schöne,
Das Heilige, das Große. Dann des Traums
Verwirklichung, auf dass das Wort ertöne.

All dies im Schatten — Strahlung oder nicht?
Will es das Schicksal, dass das Wort sich ziehe
Erlahmend durch das Leben? Fiat Lux —
Gott wollte, dass es bleibe, dass es blühe.

Ihr habt in meiner Botschaft Buch gelesen
Und fragt, woher des Meisters Stimme hallt.
Teils Shánkara, teils Krishna ist sein Wesen —
Singende Gnosis ist sein Urgehalt.

Advaita

Māyā ist eine Ausstrahlung des Ātmā,
Denn Ātmā strahlt; Es ist das Höchste Licht.
In Māyā liegen Welten mit den Zyklen —
Doch sie sind Trug, berühren Ātmā nicht.

Die Welten, Zyklen, kommen und vergehen —
Vor Ātmās Wirklichkeit kann nichts bestehen.
Was ihr erlebt von Dingen, Zeiten, Orten,
Ist Traum. Dies ist die Lehr in wenig Worten.

Indessen, Mensch: von Ātmā fiel ein Funke
Geheimnisvoll in deines Herzens Strom.
Von Māyā bleibt dein Tiefstes unverblendet —
Es ist nichts anderes als Ātmā —
Shānti Om.

Life's Work

The work, a lifelong struggle — first
Youthful dreams: the True, the Beautiful,
The Sacred, and the Great. Then dreams
Come true, that the Word might be heard.

All this amid the shadows — will it shine or not?
Does destiny wish that the Word grow weary
And weaker throughout life? *Fiat Lux* —
God willed that it should flourish and remain.

In the book of my message you have read
And ask: from whence resounds the Master's voice?
His substance is part Shankara, part Krishna —
Singing gnosis is his primordial essence.

Advaita

Māyā is radiation from *Ātmā*,
For *Ātmā* radiates: It is the Highest Light.
In *Māyā* lie the cycles of the worlds —
But they are illusions, they touch not *Ātmā*.

Worlds and cycles arise and vanish —
Before *Ātmā*'s Reality nothing endures.
What you experience of places, times, and things
Is but a dream. This is the doctrine in few words.

However, O man: from *Ātmā* fell a spark
Mysteriously into the stream of thy heart.
Thy deepest depth is not blinded by *Māyā* —
It is none other than *Ātmā* —
                              Shānti Om.

Bildnis

Pneumátikos: die Weisheit ist sein Blut;
Und dennoch: Ex Oriente Lux — das heißt:
Von Osten her kam manches hohe Wort,
Dem du verdankst, was du von Gnosis weißt.

Jedoch der Ursprung ist im Wesenskerne,
Um den sich unsere Gedanken scharen;
Der Wahrheit Blitz kommt nicht aus fremder Ferne —
Er war in unserm Herz, bevor wir waren.

Krishna

Ich möchte diesen Liederkranz vergleichen
Mit Krishnas Flöte, die von Ātmā singt.
O möge sie das harte Herz erreichen,
Das aus dem Kelch der Erdentorheit trinkt!

Da ist der Gopis goldner Liebesreigen,
Den Krishnas Spiel durchläutert und belebt;
O mög die Seel sich vor dem Zauber neigen,
Der sie befreit und zum Licht erhebt!

Portrait

Pneumátikos: Wisdom is his blood;
And yet: *Ex Oriente Lux* — which means:
Many a sacred word came from the East;
To it thou owest thy knowledge of gnosis.

But the source lies in the core of our being,
Around which our thoughts are gathered;
Truth's lightning does not come from far away —
Before we were, it was within our heart.

Krishna

I would like to compare this wreath of songs
With Krishna's flute, which sings of *Ātmā*.
O may it reach the hardened heart
That drinks of the cup of earthly folly!

There is the gopis' golden dance of love,
Made pure and vivified by Krishna's play;
O may the soul bow to the magic
That makes it free and lifts it to the Light!

Stella Matutina

Der Morgenstern erhebt sich aus der Nacht
So wie die Göttin Venus aus dem Bade
Des Meeres — eine Perle, dann ein Weib;
Urweiblich ist des Himmels Wundergnade.

Sie ist Geheimnis; sie ist nicht Gesetz,
Sie ist das freie göttliche Vergeben
Tief aus den Wassern der Unendlichkeit —

Und niemand kann der Isis Schleier heben.

Leila

Säh ich dich tanzen, Leila, wär mein Herz
Verzaubert und gebannt; zum Weg nach Innen.
Säh ich dein Antlitz, hätt ich mich vergessen —
Ich könnt mich nicht mehr auf die Welt besinnen.

Leila: der Engel der Beschaulichkeit —
Ich weiß nicht, ob du Form bist, Melodie,
Ein Liebeslied, ein goldner Märchentraum —
Oder ein Blick aus trunkner Ewigkeit.

Stella Matutina

The Morning Star rises out of the night
Like the goddess Venus from the foam
Of the sea — a pearl, and then a woman;
Profoundly feminine is Heaven's wondrous Grace.

She is mystery; she is not law,
She is free divine forgiveness,
From the deep waters of Infinity —

And none can lift the veil of Isis.

Leila

Were I to see thee dance, Leila, my heart
Would be enchanted and spellbound on its inward path.
Were I to see thy face, I would forget myself —
I could remember the world no more.

Leila: angel of contemplation —
I know not if thou art form or melody,
A love-song, a golden fairy-tale dream —
Or else a glance from drunk Eternity.

Seelenbild

Ihr müsst verstehn: ich möcht Ānanda fühlen
In allem Irdischen, das uns erquickt;
Ein Baum in Blüte, eine edle Maid,
Ein Minnelied, das unsre Seel entzückt —

Und andrerseits: ich möchte Zuflucht finden
Vor allem, was zerstreuet meinen Sinn;
O selger Stillstand fliehender Gedanken —

„O heilge Stadt Benares, die ich bin!"

Frauen

Der weise Salomo ließ Tempel bauen
Für fremde Götter, seinen lieben Frauen;
Die Magdalena goss auf Jesu Füße
Des Nardenwassers liebevolle Süße.
Auf Dantes dornenreichem Lebenspfade
Ravennas edle Frauen waren Gnade.

Das Ewig-Weibliche, ich will es loben —
Des Weibes Trost ist eine Gunst von Oben.

Soul Picture

This you must understand: I wish to feel *Ānanda*
In all refreshing earthly things:
A tree in bloom, a noble maiden,
A love-song that delights the soul.

And on the other hand: I wish to find refuge
From all distractions of the mind;
O blissful cessation of fleeting thoughts —

"O sacred city of Benares that I am!"

Women

Wise Solomon had temples built
To foreign gods, for his belovèd wives;
With loving sweetness Magdalene poured
Spikenard oil on Jesus' feet.
On Dante's thorny path of life
Ravenna's noble women were a grace.

The eternal feminine I wish to praise —
Woman's solace is a favor from Above.

Von früh

Wahrheit und Weg, dazu der Edelmut —
Dies sind die Pfeiler unsres Erdenlebens,
Auf denen alles, was wir sind, beruht;
Ohn diese Dreiheit lebt der Mensch vergebens.

Ob du nun auf des Alltags Reiz verzichtest,
Ob du der Schönheit tiefen Sinn verstehst,
Oder in beidem deine Pflicht verrichtest —
Wenn du nur treulich vor dem Höchsten stehst.

Vom frühen Morgen an musst du in Gott
Verwurzelt sein, dass deines Tages Baum
In Licht und Liebe blühe, bis zur Nacht
Wenn alles schweigt. Und Friede sei dein Traum.

Bodhisattva

Es heißt, des Bodhisattva Gnaden reichten
Weit über das gesprochne Wort hinaus —
Der Leib sei seiner Bodhi offen Haus
Und schenke uns ihr heilsverkündend Leuchten.

Geben ist seliger denn Nehmen. Strahle,
O Bodhisattva, was das Herz begehrt.
Was du mit tausendfachem Wort gelehrt,
Das gibt dein goldner Leib in einem Male.

From Early Morning

Truth, Way, then noble mind —
These are the pillars of our earthly life
Upon which rests all that we are;
Without this ternary man lives in vain.

Whether thou renounce everyday attraction,
Or understand the deep meaning of beauty,
Or accomplish thy duty in both respects —
Only stand faithfully before the Lord.

From early morning onwards thou must
Be rooted in God, that thy day's tree
May bloom in light and love till night
When all is still. And peace be thy dream.

Bodhisattva

The Bodhisattva's graces, it is said,
Extend much further than the spoken word —
His body is the open house of his Enlightenment,
Bestowing upon us its saving radiance.

To give is more blessèd than to receive.
Radiate, O Bodhisattva, what the heart desires.
What thou hast taught with a thousand words,
Thy golden body all at once bestows.

Ad astra

Ad astra — zu den Sternen — ist der Weg;
Adastra ist der Name, den ich wähle.
Mein ist der Sternenweg, und ich bin sein —
Kristall der Wahrheit und Musik der Seele.

Lichtinseln in der weiten, kalten Nacht:
Ich meine, tausendmal mein Herz zu sehen.
Weit und doch nah ist unser Weg zum Selbst —
Zur letzten Seligkeit in Gottes Höhen.

Endwort

Ein Ende nimmt das Buch, doch nicht das Singen;
Es liegt in Raum und Zeit und in den Dingen
Und ist doch raum- und zeitlos, ohn Gestalt —
Es ist des Daseins Strahlen und Gehalt.

Denn Gottes Zeichen haben ihre Rede;
Du hörst sie oder hörst sie nicht.
Tief ist sie in dein eignes Herz geschrieben —
Ein Lied von Liebe und ein Lied von Licht.

Ad Astra

Ad astra — to the stars — is the Path;
Adastra is the name I choose.
Mine is the star-path, and I belong to it —
Crystal of Truth and music of the soul.

Islands of light in cold and boundless night:
I think I see my heart a thousand times.
Far and yet near is our way to the Self —
To ultimate beatitude in God's Heights.

Last Word

The book comes to an end, but not the singing;
It lies in space and time and in all things,
And yet is spaceless, timeless, beyond form —
It is the content and radiance of our existence.

The signs of God have their own speech;
Thou hear'st it or thou hear'st it not.
This speech is written deeply in thy heart —
A song of Love, a song of Light.

Index of Foreign Quotations

Index of Titles
German and English

BY THE SAME AUTHOR

The Transcendent Unity of Religions, *1953*
Revised Edition, *1975*, *The Theosophical Publishing House, 1984, 1993*
Spiritual Perspectives and Human Facts, *1954, 1969*
New Translation, *Perennial Books, 1987*
Gnosis: Divine Wisdom, *1959, 1978, Perennial Books, 1990*
Language of the Self, *1959*, Revised Edition, *World Wisdom Books, 1999*
Stations of Wisdom, *1961, 1980*
Revised Translation, *World Wisdom Books, 1995*
Understanding Islam, *1963, 1965, 1972, 1976, 1979, 1981, 1986, 1989*
Revised Edition, *World Wisdom Books, 1994, 1998*
Light on the Ancient Worlds, *1966, World Wisdom Books, 1984*
In the Tracks of Buddhism, *1968, 1989*
New Translation, Treasures of Buddhism, *World Wisdom Books, 1993*
Logic and Transcendence, *1975, Perennial Books, 1984*
Esoterism as Principle and as Way, *Perennial Books, 1981, 1990*
Castes and Races, *Perennial Books, 1959, 1982*
Sufism: Veil and Quintessence, *World Wisdom Books, 1981*
From the Divine to the Human, *World Wisdom Books, 1982*
Christianity/Islam, *World Wisdom Books, 1985*
The Essential Writings of Frithjof Schuon (S.H. Nasr, Ed.),
1986, Element, 1991
Survey of Metaphysics and Esoterism, *World Wisdom Books, 1986, 2000*
In the Face of the Absolute, *World Wisdom Books, 1989, 1994*
The Feathered Sun: Plains Indians in Art & Philosophy,
World Wisdom Books, 1990
To Have a Center, *World Wisdom Books, 1990*
Roots of the Human Condition, *World Wisdom Books, 1991, 2002*
Images of Primordial & Mystic Beauty: Paintings by Frithjof Schuon,
Abodes, 1992
Echoes of Perennial Wisdom, *World Wisdom Books, 1992*
The Play of Masks, *World Wisdom Books, 1992*
Road to the Heart, *World Wisdom Books, 1995*
The Transfiguration of Man, *World Wisdom Books, 1995*
The Eye of the Heart, *World Wisdom Books, 1997*
Songs for a Spiritual Traveler: Selected Poems,
World Wisdom, 2002
Form and Substance in the Religions, *World Wisdom, 2002*